HERO OF THE ______ DAY?

By Henry D. Trett

ISBN: **978-1-959715-00-9**

Library of Congress Control Number: **2022948177**

Published by **Belen Books, LLC**
7901 4th St. N, Ste 300, St. Petersburg, FL. 33702 USA
Belenbookspublishing.com

Edited by Paul L. Hight & Beverly R. Waalewyn
Cover by Belen Media Group

Printed in the United States of America
41.4402° N, 123.7019° W

For L.M.M.

"Whenever you are to do a thing tho' it can never be known but to yourself, ask yourself how you would act were all the world looking at you, & act accordingly."

—Thomas Jefferson, 1785

"The media's the most powerful entity on earth. They have the power to make the innocent guilty and to make the guilty innocent, and that's power. Because they control the minds of the masses."

—Malcom X

"If I stop to help this man, what will happen to me? But… the good Samaritan reversed the question: If I do not stop to help this man, what will happen to him?"

—Martin Luther King, Jr.

HERO OF THE

_______ DAY?

Consider Yourself Warned

At the advice of legal counsel, I have been instructed to post the following warning:

♦♦♦

This book contains the details of a very specific event, divulged in chronological order. The descriptions within are based solely upon the first-hand knowledge, or the stated opinions, of the writer. Other elements of this book were compiled utilizing eye-witness accounts, published interviews, news coverage, affidavits, transcripts, depositions, court testimony, and other verified sources documenting said event.

Outside the scope of this one particular event, any resemblance to actual persons, living or dead, is purely coincidental. Furthermore, this book includes depictions of graphic violence, it contains offensive language, and it explores, what some might consider, controversial subject matter. But, as Frank Sinatra famously sang, *'That's Life'*.

So, for those of you who are easily offended by the brutal nature of life, and death, then I would recommend that you look elsewhere for your entertainment. Now, with all that unpleasantness behind us, are you sitting comfortably?

Good, then let us begin…

Man of Inconsequence

A good man should die a good death, surrounded by other good men, to be whisked away to Heaven, or Valhalla, or some other place far removed from this world. I read this in a book once, the title and author of which I had long ago forgotten. Yet, a thought sweeps over me when I am in such a mind as of today.

What of a bad man? Does he not deserve the same fate?

I mean, the only difference between a "good" man and a "bad" man is just a matter of perception. Your life experiences, subtle prejudices, and deep held emotions determine what you think of others. You, without meaning to, become the Judge, Jury, and Executioner of who is *good* and who is *bad*. So, with that ugly truth in mind, a bad man deserves the same escape from this world.

But what of a man of inconsequence? What of someone like me?

To be good or bad, a man must make his stand on top of either hill, but a man of inconsequence never makes that choice. He never loves anything, or hates anything, enough to pick a hill to climb. No, a man of inconsequence does not deserve the fate of a good, or a bad, man. He is fated to remain in this purgatory, lonely and nameless, forever stuck between those two hills. Yes, the best a man of inconsequence can hope for is to stay afloat long enough for someone, or something, to push him to pick a side. When will someone, or something, push me to decide?

Be careful of what you ask for because you just might get it.

Shall I Entertain You with A Tale of My Sweet Sorrow?

Call me David, most everyone else does. Yet, there is a vocal group of people who prefer to use more colorful terms like *Murderer*, *Killer*, and *Racist*; to name just a few examples. But my given name is David Alan Taylor, and I'd like to start with that, if you don't mind. This book is about the *incident*, as I like to call it, and offers a chronological account as told by me, the writer.

Oh, I am sure that if Tonya Jones or Dr. James Johnson had bothered to write about the *incident*, that it would look and feel very different than my perspective. That's the funny thing about perspective, it can convince two different people, who witness the exact same thing, to arrive at completely opposite conclusions. But, as it is, neither one has shown much interest in exploring the subject matter at hand. So, fortunately, or unfortunately, depending entirely upon your point of view, you are stuck with my version of the events surrounding the *incident*.

There were several things that I did know about, in real-time. Yet there were so many other things that happened without my direct knowledge, only to revealed by the universe at a later date. As a result, I've used interviews, transcripts, depositions, trial testimony, and other sources to piece together a better understanding of what happened, when it happened, and in the order of how things happened that night. And, of course, in the many days since.

Everything on the following pages is my attempt to create a more comprehensive picture of a very intricate chain of events as the *incident* extended around and, ultimately, consumed my ordinary life. It is my hope that you can learn something from my mistakes, misfortune, and struggle to understand why any of this had to happen.

This is the story of my life, at least up until this point. I'm sure you've heard all about me and what I did. It was in all the papers, on all the TV networks, and brought to you, in real time, by the trolls on the web. I'm sure you have heard the sordid details of my life from those who know me, those who think they know me, and so many of those trying to cash in on my misfortune. Sadly, one could get very rich if they peddled the preferred narrative.

Ever since the *incident*, my life has been laid out for the entire world to judge, based solely on the sound bites generated by the insatiable appetite of the media machine. So called experts telling anyone who would listen, what I did was wrong and why I shouldn't have done it.

It's easy for any simpleton to critique my actions when they have the luxury of hindsight, and hours of research studying the video, frame by frame. Personally, I would like to see how they would react in the same situation, could they step in and do what was done, or would they just sit there and watch it all happen?

Like any target of a media feeding frenzy, I have my supporters and my detractors, but I really wish they would all just go away. I am a shy person by nature and have no desire to be subjected to this level of scrutiny. I have spoken out in my defense many times but have never publicly explained what really happened behind the scenes, after the *incident*. I have never pointed out the real villains or properly thanked the true heroes, but all that changes today.

My life has been typical of most people; aside from my teenage years, you could even call it dull. I won't bore you with the day-to-day details of my life before the *incident*; anything of real importance will come up later in this book.

The first 10,957 days were fairly normal. I was born in Orlando to loving parents who went out of their way to provide for me. I played all the usual sports: football, baseball, and soccer. I was athletic but, never a standout. I went to public schools and had my share of forgettable moments. I wasn't in with the popular crowd, but I had plenty of friends. I was smart, but I didn't like school. I had dated many girls, but I never really found true love. Like everyone, I had my dirty little secrets that I kept locked safely away, or so I thought. I was a good employee, and yet I somehow managed to stay mired in mediocrity. I was a somebody, and yet a nobody at the same time.

This was the story of my life, a series of starts and stops, an exercise in futility. In fact, most of my life had been spent flying under the radar of fame or fortune; that is, until one seemingly ordinary day.

Again, there's no real point to describe the events of that day. Suffice to say that most of the day was irrelevant to the actual *incident,* honestly, not very interesting. But for those of you who are, for whatever reason, fascinated with the details of that day, I'll give you a list of events as they occurred.

It all began on a Saturday morning in November, and it was a day that began like countless others in my life. As usual, my body was up hours before my mind was ready, so I went through the motions of my morning routine in a zombie-like state. I could not shake the cobwebs out of my mind, so I had to rely on the second greatest of all inventions: coffee.

A Texas sized cup with enough cream and sugar to single handedly keep the economy rolling along smoothly. I ate a toasted bagel with light (as in a little) cream cheese while sitting on the couch in front of the TV, getting my morning news fix. The news was bad: a murder here, home invasion there, charges of political corruption in Washington, unrest in the Middle East, and the list went on and on. Yes, it was going to be another predictable day, just like any other randomly selected day from my average life.

There's no telling what will go through your mind once you jump into the shower. That morning, my mind was pondering 'life'. It's funny how time plays little tricks on you with the choices that you make. Every day decisions change the direction of your existence in an instant. Turn left instead of right, miss your plane, sleep an extra five minutes, or any one of the countless other anomalies that can happen, and your reality is irrevocably changed. Sometimes for the better, sometimes for the worse, but your life is always changed. It can keep you up late at night playing the '*What If*' game in your mind.

What if I had bought that stock at $5 a share that is now selling at $500 a share?

What if I had listened to my parents and finished college instead of dropping out and getting married?

What if I hadn't been drinking, would I have still done that? The game goes on and on, until in a moment of frustration you pop that sleeping pill, drink that bottle, or do whatever it is you do to take your mind off the game.

But how would your life be different? Would you be richer, poorer, happier, or smarter? Would you be a celebrity, a professional athlete, a criminal, or just the same person with the same problems? Would you still be just another nameless face in a sea of desperation trying to carve a life out of this fast-food World?

Who is responsible for this debacle? In a word: Fate.

Fate is a constant state of change, flowing in only one direction, pushing you from birth to death, and spinning your life out of control for all the World to see. It's enough to drive a sane person mad, and to push a mad person over the edge, but I digress.

Why did all this matter to me? Well, it was my birthday, and not just any birthday, but my 30th birthday. It's the point of no return when you magically become an adult, that point in your life when you really begin to question who you are and what you have accomplished. To be honest, I didn't like my answer to either question. I wasn't sure who I was, but I was sure of whom I was not. I was not a revolutionary, a diplomat, or a doctor. I was not a World leader, a shining example of virtues, or even a real contributing member of society. I was just another body with a social security card and a list of complaints that stood about neck high, and I had not accomplished anything either.

As a young boy, I had all these dreams about who I would be. When I grew up, I wanted to be an astronaut, a firefighter, a cowboy, the President. I wanted to be a rock star, a sports star, a star of stage and screen. I wanted all of these things and more, but somewhere along the way reality set in. There were deadlines, compromises, disappointments, and failures. My dreams were put on hold or replaced with worthless and shallow ideas of what I should be. There was no substance in my life, no driving force to propel me through the minefield that is society. I was stuck in the quagmire of mediocrity, with no way out. As depressing as all this contemplation was, I was running late so the soul searching would have to continue in the car.

My thoughts were a mess as I drove to the golf course. Was I that hopeless, or just too timid to make a change? Despite everything, I still held on to hope. Faith that things would soon change…and change for the better. The expectation that I, too, would be living the good life, always somewhere in the near future.

Someday my luck would have to change, maybe with a little help from Fate. Perhaps I should get off my ass and do something to help myself, like going back to school and finishing my master's degree. Maybe I will meet my soul mate, and we could start a family together. Who knows, I could even win the lottery. No matter how far-fetched a dream may be, as long as you hold on to hope; anything is possible. Maybe a birthday was just the very thing that I needed to revive my hopes and dreams. But I couldn't think about it anymore, it was time to play golf.

There was me, my best friend Terry, and two other people, [basically, what writers often refer to as McGuffins, or so I am told]. Yes, I know they were actual people; people that I had worked with for a couple of years, and they were there on the golf course with me that very morning. I never saw them again after that round of golf, they might as well have been figments of my imagination, how quickly they vanished from my life. Yet, that's how things work: sometimes people come, sometimes people go, but life itself just keeps moving on.

Hero of the Day?

Terry and I met through work several years ago, and over time have developed a very close friendship. Terry was just taller than me, with thick black hair and a perfect goatee accenting his impeccable taste in clothes. His prescription glasses gave him the appearance of a distinguished professor, knowledgeable and worldly. He was a character, a born salesman, with a quick wit and the gift of gab. He was the polar opposite of my quiet, almost brooding, personality.

As we were walking up to the first tee, Terry asked, "The usual bet?"

The usual bet was a dollar per hole, loser buys lunch. Not big stakes by any means, but for two very competitive men, it might as well have been a million dollars on the line for all we cared. Terry was the better golfer than I was, but, fortunately, the game of golf had found a way to equal things out: the handicap. Per previously negotiated terms, worked out during a heavy night of drinking, Terry spotted me the customary stroke for each hole played. But on that particular day, I would ask, "How about five extra strokes?"

Terry laughed, "Yeah, sure. It's your birthday, why the fuck not?"

As we walked up to the tee, I stated, "Ladies first…"

McGuffin #1 hit the golf ball two hundred forty yards, but wide right of the fairway. McGuffin #2 hit his golf ball two hundred sixty yards to the left side of the fairway. Terry drove his ball two hundred seventy yards, slightly right of center. Me, I crushed my tee-shot some two hundred fifty yards, right down the middle; oh yeah, it was going to be a good day.

♦♦♦

That's the funny thing about golf, how much it resembles life. It all looks so simple from afar, but things can get so complicated, so messy, so quickly. Just a slight hitch in your swing, and the ball flies wildly out of control. Life works in much the same way. A slight twitch from Fate, and your life spirals wildly out of balance. And maddening, don't forget how maddening golf, and by extension, life, can be. Yet, you can hack your way around a golf course, or life, and still get lucky every once in a while. Or not, it never seemed to be quite fair when you factored in the cruelty of Fate. But there was always one shot, maybe two, that were perfect over the course of eighteen holes, just enough to keep you coming back for more. Life, or so it seemed, followed the same pattern.

I ended the day with a true ninety, enough to win the round against Terry. It was amazing, the weather was ideal, the ball stayed in the fairway, and I managed to make some great putts. It really helped to lift my spirits. Beating Terry at anything always lifted my spirits. Yeah, did I mention that I am a competitive person?

After a round of golf, almost nothing is better than good food and lots of beer. We sat around drinking and laughing about this shot and that shot, who had the longest drive, and many other stupid tests of manhood. It is times like these that I feel the most comfortable; the camaraderie, the laughter, and the friendships that cannot be bought or sold. For those of you who do care, I had a turkey sandwich and drank four beers.

Yeah, yeah, I know, you're not supposed to drink and drive, but it was one of those things I had learned to do over the years. We *ALL* do things that we shouldn't do. As usual, I went out of my way to take back roads and avoid the police. I had the stereo blaring and was singing along to the music. I sound terrible when I sing; however, no one was there to hear me, so it was okay for me to make a complete ass out of myself. There's something about a good beer buzz that just gets you moving. You should know what I mean, and for those of you who don't, try to live a little.

The first thing I did when I walked in the door was to hit the bathroom. I don't know about you, but beer runs through me like water through a sieve. The second thing I did was crack open another beer. Then I stripped off my shirt, shoes, and socks while heading for the pool. Even in Florida the water is a little too cold to go swimming in November; but the weather is perfect for sitting outside by the pool. On most days, the sun shines bright with hardly a cloud in the sky, while the daytime temperature is a comfortable mid 60's to low 70's. It makes living through the scorching Florida summers worthwhile.

That Saturday was no exception. The temperature on the patio was a pleasant 71 degrees with a cloudless blue-sky overhead. I turned on the radio, drank about half my beer, and fell asleep in the hammock.

Meet the Parents

I awoke to the sound of a ringing phone; on the line were my parents. They were wondering why I had not called them yet so they could wish me a happy birthday. I used the lame excuse of being so busy that I just didn't have the time to call. When, in reality, I was just sleeping.

Mom and Dad were a shining example of a dysfunctional relationship at its best. On the surface everything looked immaculate, but if you ventured into the shadows, you could see the stress fractures of reality. After thirty-one years of marriage, you would think that my parents would be beyond ignoring the obvious. Granted, Mom and Dad meant well, they just had their share of problems.

Dad was a good-looking chap with thick, mostly blondish hair. Although Dad only stood 5'10", he seemed like a giant when I was growing up. A solid jaw line and quick temper were hallmarks of the Taylor lineage. Robust and outgoing, he had one major weakness: women. Mom pretended not to notice his extra-marital affairs; maybe she was just too afraid of being alone. When Dad wasn't busy at late night "meetings", he was fishing. He tried to introduce me to the regal sport, but I just couldn't get past the slimy feel of fish.

Mom always had a certain aura about her. Confident and calculating, she knew the right words for any occasion. At 5'2", my mother was a little dynamo who could accomplish anything with the slightest of ease. Mom, being very conscious of her looks, worked very hard to keep her hair blonde and her body tight. She spent hours in the gym and kept regular appointments with Brendan, the '*famous*' hairstylist in Winter Park.

Perfection was the order of the day, and yet, Mom had a terrible secret; she smoked. Of course, everyone knew the truth, but my mom did her best to hide the habit from friends and family. Dad detested smoking, which was a little surprising considering his years spent as a smoker. Although he never mentioned it directly to my mom, I heard about it frequently.

Growing up the way I did, one tends to get a little jaded; I was no exception. Mom lying to Dad about smoking, Dad lying to Mom about his secretary; it was all so confusing for a child. By the time I was in high school I believed that all the deception, in an otherwise normal life was, well, *normal*. I became an emotional introvert, keeping my feelings hidden from everyone including myself. Add in the occasional failed relationship, and you have a recipe for disaster.

When the time was right, I headed off to college. Once there, my parents became a distant memory. I rarely came home, and when I did, I spent all my time with friends. Not that my parents noticed, I mean Dad with his fishing and his secretary, and Mom with her workouts; they didn't have the free time anyway.

This pattern continued, even after I graduated and moved back to Orlando. Over time I grew to understand, and even appreciate my parents. After all, you should always love your parents, faults, and all, and I love mine. Now we would get together on holidays and special occasions, today being one of those special occasions. I repeat, I do love my parents, but they have this strange fetish with eating dinner before 6:00 PM. It makes me nuts that they have to eat so early, but here I was rushing to get ready and make it to the restaurant before six so my parents could eat. It's a quick shower, a quick shave, and then a mad dash to the bedroom and find something to wear. Before you know it, I was running out the door.

As usual, my parents were there long before I showed up. To make matters worse, they couldn't be seated until the entire dining party was present. All I could do was shrug and say I'm sorry. It sounded insensitive then, and honestly, time hasn't improved my response any. At least I had time to order a drink from the bar.

Barney's Steakhouse is one of those places that every town has, a hidden gem amongst the neon lights of this cookie-cutter world. It was a place that only the locals knew about, although it's been around forever, and the food's pretty damn good. The decor, on the other hand, had seen better days. Outside, the building was plain and uninspiring, nothing to indicate the quality of the food they served. The inside of the restaurant was done in a 70's type decor emphasizing dark wood and poor lighting to set an intimate mood.

That night, however, wasn't about a romantic evening for two; it was a celebration of sorts, honoring the achievement of a significant milestone in life. Lucky me. Oh yeah, for you curious types, I had the sirloin tips with mashed potatoes and fresh green beans. I also had three more beers to wash it all down.

I said my goodbyes and thanked my parents for dinner. With the obligatory parent time now out of the way, I would soon be downtown, and my date with destiny. I had that good beer buzz going again and I just knew that this night would be one for the annuals.

While driving, my mind was considering all the possibilities of the upcoming evening. A thousand different scenarios were playing out in my head; none of which even remotely touched on the impending magnitude of the *incident*. Honestly, I was just hoping to get laid; I had no other ambitions, or desire, to be involved with such an infamous event.

♦♦♦

It's always hard to find a parking spot downtown, so imagine my surprise when, on the second level of the parking garage, I found a spot right next to the elevator. I remember thinking to myself that this was a good sign of things to come.

It had been previously decided that I would rendezvous with some friends around 8:00 PM downtown to properly celebrate my birthday. For once in my life, I was actually early and ended up having to wait for everyone else to show up. So, I ordered another beer. For those of you counting at home, that's eight and a half beers thus far, including the three from dinner.

Remember before when I said that we *ALL* do things that we shouldn't? Well, we also lie to protect someone else's feelings or to save a relationship that would be destroyed by a simple truth. At the time, it seems like the decent thing to do.

You should try to help others and, sometimes, deflect blame to protect yourself.

A little misdirection here, a half-truth there, and usually everything works out just fine. Most people don't stop to check the facts; they want to believe a plausible story. But every once in a while, *BOOM!* It all blows up in your face. Friendships are lost forever, and relationships are destroyed by a white lie meant to obscure an uncomfortable reality.

The sad truth is, usually, if we had just come clean in the first place, the whole disaster may have been averted. It's impossible to achieve, but no one ever wants to admit to being less than perfect; no one ever wants to admit just how weak and selfish we really are. So, you go about your life pretending not to notice the figurative mines you've laid; you don't bother to write down their locations because it's safer to keep that information in your mind and not on paper for the world to see.

You're optimistic and think that bad things only happen to other people, and never to you; so, you ignore the danger lurking right under your very nose. You know it's an explosive situation, but somehow, you've become complacent and think you've got it all under control. Besides, how bad could it actually be, it's not like you've killed someone, right?

Average, everyday ordinary people don't have big problems; they just have a lot of little annoyances. At least they look little from the surface, but just like an iceberg, you never really know how deep they go until it is too late. Little did I realize how big of a powder keg that I was sitting on, just how soon it would explode, and what the ramifications would be.

♦♦♦

The first to show up was Robyn. To me, Robyn was perhaps the most beautiful woman that I had ever seen. At 5'3" and barely a hundred pounds, Robyn had the attitude of a Titan. Long sandy blonde hair and eyes the color of a good scotch splashed with a hint of brilliant green; Robyn had always seemed beyond my reach. Marriage had tamed her spirit a tad, but she still possessed a lust for life that could be so intoxicating. Before, when I said that I had not found true love, I lied; it's just that she belonged to someone else.

Now I feel I need to explain the Robyn situation, so there is no confusion. Yes, Robyn and I *did* date at one time, but we found that we were much better friends than lovers (one of those white lies). Yes, we did 'hook up' from time-to-time, even when we were dating other people. Yes, we did go to Las Vegas, as a couple, only a week before she was married. Yes, we secretly stayed in contact via the telephone despite her husband's demand that she never talk to me again. Yes, we would occasionally go out to lunch together, about once every month or so, and yes, I would lie about the nature of our relationship to protect her.

We still flirted with each other, but ever since Robyn's marriage, our relationship had stayed strictly friends. Robyn loved her husband very much and would not do anything to hurt him. That said, she still felt a strong connection to me and, for some stupid reason, could not bring herself to give me up as a friend.

It was not a relationship that could be easily explained, or understood, by others; and as such, we just found it easier to keep our relationship a private matter. So, there were times, like that night, when she would tell her husband a little white lie so she could spend time with me. That night, Robyn had told Tom that she and some friends from work were going to meet downtown and have a 'girl's night out'.

Next to show up was one of my childhood friends, Chris, and his wife Lynn. We all went to school together, but it wasn't until a few years after graduation that they got together and eventually married. They had two children now: Steve, a boy that was six years old, and Tara, an eighteen-month-old girl. Although we didn't see each other as much as we would like (it's hard having a family and a social life, or so they tell me), we still kept in contact on a regular basis.

Two weeks before my birthday, Chris made a point of calling me and setting up the whole evening to celebrate my achievement. Of my friends from high school, Chris was the closest one that I had remained in contact with. Most of my high school friends just drifted off and did their own thing, still others packed up and moved away, but not Chris.

Of those still left in Orlando, I was the oldest, and therefore, the first to reach thirty. But, as fate would have it, of my high school friends, Chris would be the only one able to make it out that evening. Standing nearly 6 feet tall, with white-blonde hair and green eyes, Chris had a striking face and a personality that made him irresistible to women.

Despite this unfair advantage over the rest of us, he was a humble man. Well-grounded emotionally, Chris had spent his life in pursuit of the perfect woman. He was not interested in the conquest of cheap one-night stands that most men aspire to commit.

Enter Lynn, a high school acquaintance of ours, who pursued Chris for years. She was younger than us, and, in high school, that made a big difference. Once she graduated, though, Chris realized that she could be the one. Lynn was tall for a girl, just a little bit shorter than Chris, with beautiful dark brown hair and matching eyes that could penetrate even the iciest of hearts.

As usual, last to show up was Terry. After a few drinks, we decided to move on to a new bar that had just opened a couple of blocks down the street on Orange Avenue.

Meanwhile, in another universe, just six blocks away…

Diane's Dirty Little Secret

I am not the only one in this tale that had a secret to hide; Diane also had a real big secret that she was trying to cover up. Twenty minutes before we left the bar, Diane and Craig had left another downtown bar and headed for a parking garage. Diane was a fiery redhead with deep green eyes and a thirst for adventure.

Craig, on the other hand, was a bit more timid, and applied an academic approach to life, but when it came to Diane, Craig just couldn't seem to control himself. With wavy brown hair and glasses, Craig, not being a bad looking fellow, was in way over his head.

As they walked hand in hand, it looked as if another couple in love were heading into the night. Yet, in reality, Diane was heading to Craig's house for a little action, if you know what I mean. Somehow, I didn't think that her husband, Jack, would appreciate the late-night tryst.

Jack and Diane were high school sweethearts growing up in a small town, just south of nowhere in Indiana. Jack wanted to be a football star, and Diane just wanted to be anywhere but in Indiana. Jack was a talented quarterback and was recruited by several major colleges, but the key to signing Jack was Diane.

When the University of Southern California accepted Diane, Jack signed the very next day to play his college football as a Trojan. When her friends and family asked her why she wanted to go to a school on the west coast, all she could say was that it was about as far away from Indiana as she could get without leaving the continental United States.

His freshman year began with him sitting on the bench as the backup quarterback, until an injury to Roy Jones, the starting quarterback, forced Jack onto the college football stage. The Trojans won their last three games thanks, in no small part, to Jack's sheer determination and undeniable skill. By the end of the season, people were already talking about Jack as a possible Heisman Trophy candidate.

During Jack's sophomore year, he played brilliantly, and moved the Trojans to within one play shy of competing for the national championship. He didn't win the Heisman that year, but he definitely was the leading contender going into his junior year. His junior season began where his sophomore year left off, with Jack amazing the college sports world with his leadership ability and a knack for throwing the ball. Everything was going great, until the fifth game of the season.

As Jack was fighting for unnecessary extra yards, he was tackled awkwardly and tore his left knee up. After the tackle, and while he laid on the field, the injury did not look that bad. However, after the game, medical tests showed the true extent of damage done; he would be out for the remainder of the season.

Jack had the surgery and worked hard the entire next year, striving to once again play at the same level that he was accustomed to playing. When his senior year began, all the coaches felt that Jack looked better than ever and were confident that his injury would not pose a problem.

For the first eight games he played above and beyond anyone's expectations until, once again fighting for extra yards, Jack was tackled and injured again. This time Jack had his right leg severely broken, in two separate places. The injury was another heart-breaking season ender for the kid who could have been the next Joe Montana.

Jack fought hard and completed his college degree, but he never was able to regain the mobility he needed to compete in the NFL. It was a terrible waste of pure talent; but instead of being bitter, Jack focused his efforts on being successful in the business world. Jack and Diane were married six months after graduating college and moved to Orlando to follow a career offer for Jack.

In the years since college, Jack had indeed become a successful businessman. He was able to provide everything that Diane had ever wanted, a beautiful home, disposable income, and all the other trappings of a financially secure lifestyle. Jack was an adoring husband and never denied Diane any luxury or desire, but somehow it just wasn't enough for Diane. She still needed something more.

Enter Craig. Although Craig was several years her junior, he had a certain something that Diane just couldn't describe. There was an instant attraction, and that attraction turned to flirting, and flirting turned into brief moments of sexual excess. It was nothing against Jack. Diane knew he was a wonderful guy; however, Craig made Diane feel something that Jack had not be able to do in years. Craig made Diane feel sixteen again.

Craig and Diane crossed the street and headed toward the elevator leading up to her car. As the elevator door closed, they embraced and shared a passionate kiss, lasting until the elevator doors opened again. They continued kissing as they spilled out of the elevator and onto the parking garage concourse.

There was a strong smell in the air, something Diane was all too familiar with; someone was smoking a joint. It was then that Craig and Diane realized they were not alone in the parking garage. They turned to face four young black men standing off to the side of the elevator. Instinctively, Craig tried to push Diane back into the elevator car but, by now, the elevator doors were shut.

"What the fuck's your problem?" the tallest man growled. "Are you scared of me? You fucking should be!"

He abruptly pulled his jacket to one side, revealing a 9mm handgun tucked into his waistband. His friends began to slowly encircle Craig and Diane.

"Give me your fucking money!" The gun was now in his hand, and he was pointing it directly at Craig's face. Without hesitation, Craig reached into his back pocket and handed over his wallet.

The man with the gun, hissed, "The purse too, bitch!"

Diane handed over her purse without saying a word.

The man, unmoving, growled, "Now the jewelry!"

Diane struggled to remove her wedding ring and earrings, and then handed them over with a terror induced, shaking hand. The man with the gun then turned his attention back to Craig and said, "Nice watch. Now, fucking hand it over!"

It was at this point Craig…hesitated. His nice watch was a gift, two weeks ago, from Diane, and he had no intention of giving it up. Without saying another word, the man with gun took the weapon and slammed it against Craig's face. Craig fell to the ground, bleeding profusely from the mouth.

Up until this point, the other three men had done nothing, but now with Craig on the ground, two of the three began kicking and punching Craig for what seemed like an eternity. When Diane tried to intervene, the guy with the gun backhanded her, slamming her into the elevator door. She slowly slid down its stainless-steel exterior, her ears ringing, and a warm sensation was flowing from her nose.

The man with the gun reached down and removed the watch from Craig's bloody and twitching body. Then, without a word, the men left using the parking garage stairs to escape. As they left, another person, unseen by Diane or Craig, and already on the stairs, headed down with them. The man with the gun rifled through Diane's purse. After taking out her wallet, he stuffed it in his jacket pocket and then dropped the purse on the staircase before leaving the parking garage.

As the perpetrators exited the parking garage, they headed left across the street, through the drive-thru lanes of the bank.

Little CJ asked, "What the fuck was that about?"

Little CJ wasn't exactly little; he was just over six feet tall. No, it wasn't his size that earned Curtis Jones his street name; it was his older brother, Calvin Jones, who had the same initials, same looks, and had been labeled "CJ". Although only seventeen, and the youngest member of the group, Little CJ, with his cropped hair and sculpted face, could have easily been mistaken for a man in his late twenties.

Calvin Jones, CJ, was only twenty-two, but he had already experienced more violence than any man twice his age. At 6'4" and weighing more the 230 pounds, CJ was a terrifying combination of ambition and rage. CJ's response was cold, harsh, and dripping with hatred.

"They didn't show me any respect. They see a brotha and they get scared. I'm not putting up with that shit."

The third member of the group was William Baker, aka "Willie B". At the ripe old age of twenty-four, Willie B was the oldest of the group. Also a veteran of the streets, Willie B was very capable of harming anyone who he felt deserving of such punishment. Standing a respectable six feet tall, Willie B was the flamboyant one of the group. Sporting a red jacket and shoulder length dreadlocks, he was an unmistakable figure.

Willie B said, "We've got to get home, now!"

Home was on the other side of I-4, and they only had two choices; go through the crowds on Church Street or try to avoid them and go down Amelia. CJ said, "Look, we've got to split up. They might be looking for a large group of us."

The fourth member of the group, Marcus Porter, was a rotund fellow with a legendary appetite for food. As a joke, people started calling him 'Tiny', and the name stuck. Not a hardened criminal, Tiny always seemed to be in the wrong place, at the wrong time, and with the wrong people. Tonight, was no exception.

The fifth, and final, member of the group was Theo Roberts, aka "T". Like Willie B and CJ, T was also an experienced thug. Yet, unlike Willie B and CJ, T was more calculating, and profit driven. What had just happened was a complete disaster in his mind.

"Yeah, but which way do we go?" asked T.

"Let's go through the crowds and maybe they won't find us. Little CJ and me will follow you, Willie B, and Tiny."

And with that, they split up into two separate groups and headed up to Orange Avenue, turning south toward Church Street.

Diane's Lie

Diane painfully crawled over to Craig. He was barely conscious, oozing blood from his mouth and nose. Wiping the blood from her nose, Diane asked, "Craig, are you okay?"

There was no reply. She gathered her thoughts for a moment and remembered that Craig had his cell phone in his pocket. She found the phone and called 911. After a couple of rings, she heard a calm voice methodically say, "Nine-One-One Operator, what is your emergency?"

A frantic Diane said, "There's been a robbery, someone's hurt please send an ambulance!"

"What happened?" asked the operator.

Now Diane was in a spot, she couldn't tell the truth, because then Jack would know what was going on. So, she had to think of something quick, "I was robbed on the ground floor of the parking garage by four black guys. Before they left, one of them said something about some poor bastard on the third floor.

I came up the stairs and found a coworker who has been beaten very badly."

"Ma'am, what parking garage are you at?" the operator asked.

"On the corner of Rosalind and Robinson," Diane replied.

"Ma'am, are you okay?" the operator calmly asked.

"I'm a little shaken up, but Craig looks real bad. Please hurry with an ambulance. I don't think he's going to make it," a hysterical Diane cried.

"Help is on the way. Tell me, is your coworker still breathing?" the operator continued.

Diane listened carefully; she could hear Craig softly gasping for breath. "Yes, yes, he is. But he is bleeding real badly from his head and mouth."

"Now listen to me, it is real important that you do not try to move him. Help will be there soon. I'll stay with you on the phone until the ambulance arrives. They should be there soon," the operator instructed.

Still crying, Diane said, "Yeah, I hear the sirens now. Hurry! Please tell them we're on the third floor."

"I've already given them that information, ma'am. Just hang on, everything will be alright" the operator replied.

The wailing of an approaching siren drowned out whatever noise Diane could initially hear in the parking garage. Although it had been just a few minutes, it felt like hours had passed since she first reached out for help. However, in the brief silence of the siren cycle, Diane thought that she heard a strange noise growing louder.

For some odd reason, it sounded like bike tires on pavement reverberating within the concrete surrounding her. Just as she began to question her own sanity, a man in uniform rounded the corner. Diane sighed in relief, "I see a police officer. Thank you, thank you so much!"

"You're welcome. Everything is going to be okay. The ambulance is just a couple of minutes away," the operator continued.

♦♦♦

Officer Mike Thomas was the first person to arrive on the scene. A tall muscular man, Officer Thomas kept his dark hair closely shaved to hide the thinning patch on the crown of his head. Even clad in the traditional "Bike Cop" uniform of tight black shorts and matching collar shirt, Officer Thomas was still an imposing figure.

When the call came in, he had only been a few blocks to the south, on the far side of Lake Eola. He knew exactly where the parking garage was and headed there immediately for the people in distress. As he rapidly biked his way to the location, he kept his eye out for anything, or anyone, out of the ordinary, but he never saw a thing.

As he rolled up the garage to the third floor, he tried to prepare himself for whatever might be waiting. He was aware that someone had been hurt, but he wouldn't know how badly, or what type of injuries had been sustained until he got there.

Upon rounding the corner, he saw a woman clutching a cell phone with one hand and using the other to rub the back of the victim. Something inside told him that there was more to the story than what had been reported by the 911 operator. In a calm, reassuring manner, Officer Thomas asked, "Are you okay?"

"I'll be alright, but I'm afraid Craig's gonna die," Diane gasped.

Looking at Craig, Officer Thomas realized that the injuries were quite severe. However, his police training knew that the truth would only exacerbate the situation, so he told

Diane a little white lie, “I’m sure he’ll be fine. Look, here comes the ambulance now.”

The ambulance rounded the corner and pulled to an abrupt stop. Two men climbed out and headed for the back of the ambulance. From there they pulled out some medical equipment and quickly approached Craig. One stopped to look at Diane; using a flashlight, he checked her eyes, asked a few basic questions, and then stated, “You’re going to be okay.”

Officer Mike Thomas spoke up, “Can I ask her some questions?”

“Yeah. Just please move her away from here so we can work on this guy,” whispered the EMT.

As the EMTs continued to assist Craig, Officer Thomas moved Diane past the elevator, and just out of sight from the medical team, “Can you please tell me what happened?”

Diane started her story, “I was leaving a bar down the street when I was accosted by four young black men on the ground floor of the parking garage. The tall one flashed a gun, took my purse, and fled with his friends. As they left, someone said something about me being luckier than someone else upstairs.”

“How long ago did this happen?” Officer Thomas asked.

She hesitated, "I don't know, not very long. Maybe ten minutes ago."

Officer Thomas, taking notes, continued his interrogation, "Can you describe the robbers?"

Diane said, "Yeah. There were four of them, all tall and black. The one thing I remember the most, is that one guy was wearing a red jacket with dreadlocks."

Officer Thomas pressed Diane for more information, "A red jacket? Dreadlocks? Was there anything else you can remember about the others?"

"Yeah, the gun was real big," Diane answered.

Just to see Diane's expression, Officer Thomas asked, "So at what point did you go upstairs?"

This question caught Diane off-guard; it took her a few seconds to remember her own white lie, "I went upstairs after the men were out of sight."

Seeing Diane's surprised expression and hesitation, Officer Thomas decided to keep digging, "What direction did they head?"

"They left across the street to the right," Diane stammered.

"So instead of trying to find help on the street you decided to go upstairs *alone*?" Officer Thomas persisted with his line of questioning.

"Yeah, I wanted to be sure that no one else was hurt or anything," Diane replied, trying to recover from her mental mistake.

"So, once you go upstairs and then you find…" Officer Thomas said while pointing in the direction of Craig.

"Craig, yeah. He was laying there in a pool of his own blood," Diane responded.

Officer Thomas asked, "It was then that you called nine-one-one?"

With Diane's confidence in her cover story regaining momentum, she said, "Yeah, they took my phone with my purse, but I knew Craig from work, and knew that he carried a cell phone too; so, I went and looked for it in his pockets. It was then I called nine-one-one."

A hollow voice came through Office Thomas' radio.

"Excuse me for one minute," Thomas said while he stepped back a couple of steps. Then, he relayed the information he had learned about the crime and the perpetrators, as more police arrived on the scene.

Let The Games Begin

When we decided to leave the bar, we had to wait for the bartender to close out our tab. After five minutes of waiting, Chris sent us ahead to grab a spot at the next bar. Less than a minute after our departure, the bartender showed up with our tab in hand. Chris signed off on the charges, collected his credit card, and headed for the door with Lynn. This slight delay spared Chris and Lynn a front row seat to the carnage that was about to unfold.

For those keeping score, I had four more beers before leaving the club. That brings my total beer consumption up to twelve and a half for the day, seven since six that evening. A lot by anybody's standards, and on any other day you would be right; but after all, it was my thirtieth birthday. Didn't I deserve to have a little fun?

One minute, one way or another, and it wouldn't have mattered. It would have been just another night in the life of my ordinary existence; my drinking never would have become an issue. But I can say this, without any doubt, that if I had been sober, I certainly never could have, nor would have, had the nerve to do what I was about to do.

Officer Paul Rodriguez was just one of the many Orlando Police Officers working the downtown area that night. Just under six-feet tall and cursed with a boyish face, Officer Rodriguez wasn't what you would consider an authority figure. With his black hair slicked back and his neatly trimmed moustache, Officer Rodriguez did not look dangerous to anybody. But once in uniform, and armed with a 9mm police issued firearm, Officer Rodriguez was a force to be reckoned with.

He was near the corner of Orange and Church when he got the call about a pair of violent armed robberies a few blocks away. Just a few minutes later, he spotted a group of three black men turn west on Church Street from Orange Avenue. It wasn't the right number of perpetrators—or *perps* as law enforcement often called them—that OPD was looking for; but one of them had dreadlocks and was wearing a red jacket.

Officer Rodriguez fell in behind the trio and began following them as they moved toward I-4. He asked for a more accurate description, but none was available. Officer Rodriguez was now about ten feet behind the trio when he spotted what appeared to be a bulge on the back right side of the jacket that resembled a gun. Immediately, Officer Rodriguez pulled out his side arm and requested back up.

As Fate would have it, I was walking in the other direction, on Officer Rodriguez' right hand side, just a couple of feet away when I noticed that he had his gun out. I had just nudged Terry to show him the situation when *BOOM!* The echo of a single gunshot ricocheted through the brisk night air, and everyone in a one-block radius, with the exception of five people, hit the ground.

It was only later that we would find out that CJ and Tiny had been communicating the position and stance of Officer Rodriguez. When I looked up from the ground, I saw Officer Rodriguez lying face down in the street, just a couple of feet in front of me. I also saw CJ calmly stroll up and straddle the wounded officer. And there, just to my left, was Officer Rodriguez's firearm. What CJ said next was a matter of debate; I thought that I heard him clearly and calmly say, "Time to die, cop."

Other people swear that they heard CJ say something to the effect of, "Do you want to die cop?"

Either way, it didn't look good for the unresponsive Officer. As CJ was slowly extended his gun, pointing it at the back of Officer Rodriguez's head, I was thinking that I should do something.

What happened next took place in the span of ten seconds. *Ten fucking seconds*, from start to finish! Just think about that! There are approximately 31,536,000 seconds that elapse for every calendar year. Can you imagine squeezing all of your morality, your whole existence, into just ten fucking seconds? But there I was weighing my options: do I get involved and place myself in harm's way, or do I play it safe? Do I stay on the sidelines and just let it all happen?

I was drunk, so what do you think I did?

Stupid me, I picked up the gun and strolled up to CJ from the back, and to the right, so that I was just outside his line of sight. Without saying a word, I fired the gun. The sound was deafening. The bullet entered CJ's head just below his right ear and exploded out just above his left eye. CJ slowly dropped to his knees and fell to the left, over and on top of the unconscious Officer Rodriguez.

A halo of dark blood began to gather and expand around the remains of CJ's head. I had never fired a real gun before in my life; I had used BB guns and air rifles as a kid, but nothing ever like this. I expected a big kick from the recoil, but to my amazement, the gun hardly moved at all.

Now, I have heard that time seems to stand still in a stressful situation like this. All sounds seem to disappear, and you feel as if your feet are made of concrete. I guess the only thing that I can think of to compare this type of close-range combat to, is an unavoidable car accident.

There you are, traveling at 100 MPH, and you see that brick wall ahead; you see it coming at you, you know it's there, you know that you are going to hit it, so you brace yourself for the upcoming impact. Yes, you prepare, but deep in your soul, you know that there is absolutely nothing you can do to stop it. Anyway, that's how I felt after the first shot was fired. I remember every detail, every sight, every smell, every sensation, but surprisingly, I don't remember any sound.

I was now pointing the gun at Little CJ, not sure what to do next. Little CJ's mouth gaped open and let out what witnesses would later describe as a combination of rage and terror. As soon as he moved in my direction, I pulled the trigger again. The impact of the bullet pushed him backward; he fell on his back, arms outstretched landing on the ground with his right leg slightly over his left. He never moved again.

It was too late now; I had passed the point of no return. I spun to my right and faced the three remaining combatants. I remember, very distinctly, the look of sheer terror on Willie B's face as I fired another round that sailed wide, and left, of his head. He was struggling, trying to remove his gun from behind his back, when I fired my next shot. It was a clean hit, striking Willie B just below his Adam's apple, driving his body down to the ground, and out of sight.

Then I felt a most curious sensation, almost like a red-hot poker had been rammed through my right shoulder; at the time it didn't register to me that I had just been shot by Tiny. I methodically moved my aim a little to the right, and fired two more shots in rapid succession, striking Tiny twice in the chest. Tiny's second and final shot sailed wide left of my head. And then it happened again; only this time I felt like my left thigh had just been struck with a 20lb sledgehammer, and I couldn't stop myself from falling to my knees.

I looked at the last man standing, T, and saw a flash from his gun and felt the sledgehammer hit me again. The impact caused me to fire a shot that ricocheted off the ground and eventually struck a building two blocks down. After the last impact, I felt my gaze turn skyward, and I could feel myself collapsing over backward. I wasn't aware of it at the time, but when I hit the ground, I fired one last shot that apparently struck T as he was turning to flee. The final shot of this Wild West drama entered T's back and lodged in his lower spine.

So now there I was, lying on top of CJ's feet and over Officer Rodriguez's back, looking up at the night sky. I remember thinking how beautiful the stars looked from this vantage point. The pain I felt was so intense, the damage to my body so severe, that I was sure this breathtaking natural artistic masterpiece would be the last thing that I would ever see.

It was at this moment when my hearing slowly came back to me. At first it was muffled and vague, but within seconds I could clearly hear the screams of panic from the horrified witnesses. And even more disturbing to me, I could hear myself moaning and gasping for breath.

I remember thinking, I know I'm going to die tonight. I had made my peace with it; I had accepted my fate. There was, ultimately, no one to blame but myself for this predicament.

I was starting to fade from consciousness, when a sharp and determined voice yelled at me, *"Drop the fucking gun!"*

I opened my eyes, and then made visual contact with Officer Debra Johnson. Officer Johnson was a black woman in her late thirties. She was not fat, but thick, if you know what I mean.

She repeated her command, *"Drop the fucking gun, now!"*

I tried to speak, but could only manage a feeble whisper, "I can't feel my hand."

Officer Johnson used her right foot to apply pressure on my limp left hand, all the while still pointing her firearm directly at my forehead. When my hand finally opened, she reached down with her left hand, and pulled the gun out of reach.

Officer Johnson was one of two OPD officers responding to Officer Rodriguez's request for backup. Unbeknownst to me, or any of the others involved with the shooting, Officer Johnson was only a hundred or so feet to the west of the confrontation when the first shot was fired. She actually was close enough to see me shoot CJ and the others, but because of the large number of civilians in-between us, she was unable to fire her weapon.

After retrieving the gun, she called for ambulances and more backup on the radio. Then, she began the gruesome task of checking CJ and Little CJ for vital signs. Now, that I was awake again, I took the opportunity to look around the area. There were bodies everywhere, and so much blood. More blood than I could have ever imagined.

Underneath me, I could feel Officer Rodriguez start to cough, spit, and shake as he started to regain consciousness. Upon hearing the gasping of fallen Officer Rodriguez, Officer Johnson simultaneously reached over, grabbed me by the collar, and yanked my body off to reveal a very bloody, stunned, and confused OPD officer.

Officer Doug Johnson, no relation to Officer Debra Johnson, was the second officer responding to the request for backup. A large man with a baldhead and bright yellow tufts around the side and back, he was just a few dozen yards east of the confrontation when the first shot was fired. Because of the large Saturday night crowd, he wasn't able to see what was happening, but within seconds, he was hearing multiple gunshots and he knew that something terrible was unfolding in the very near distance.

I'm sure that it must have been so frustrating for Officer Johnson having to dodge fleeing civilians, and it must have left him feeling helpless as the final shots rang out. I wouldn't know, as the two of us had never actually spoken about that night with one another.

Officer Johnson barreled his way through the escaping masses and suddenly he was there, literally spilling onto the scene. In front of him there were three people down. The man on his left was face down on the sidewalk, desperately trying to crawl away. All that effort, but, literally, going nowhere.

The man in the middle was lying on his back; arms at his side with his left leg curled up like a flamingo. His whole body suddenly started to convulse, and, in a matter of seconds, it stopped, and then started again. The man to the right was on the ground, using both hands in a futile attempt to stop the blood gushing out of his neck. His legs were moving back and forth, like he was trying to kick an imaginary soccer ball.

Officer Rodriguez was now on his hands and knees coughing, trying to catch his breath. A female voice cried out somewhere in the chaos: *"I'm a nurse, let me help!"* Then another voice continued, *"So am I!"*

Amid the carnage, more and more police were arriving, trying to separate the curious onlookers from the dead and dying. The sounds of multiple sirens making their way to the scene echoed between the city buildings. One of the nurses came up to first look at CJ, someone in the crowd said, "There's no point, he's got no fucking head left."

Ignoring the obvious diagnosis, she bent down and soon realized the extent of the damage caused by the bullet; there was no hope of saving him. The nurse then turned her attention to Little CJ; she felt for a pulse and then began to perform CPR. She worked feverously trying to revive the young man, but he too was lost forever.

Using her blood-stained hands, she gently closed his lifeless eyes.

On the other side of the disaster, a second nurse applied pressure on Willie B's neck, trying to stop him from bleeding to death. She asked an Officer for a shirt, a handkerchief, something to try and slow the bleeding. From somewhere in the crowd, a shirt came flying in her direction. She immediately wadded it up and applied it to the gaping wound and instructed the nearest person to hold the makeshift bandage in place so she could check on the others.

She moved over to Tiny, whose body was again convulsing. She talked to him in a calm voice, asking him to just hang in there, telling him that help was on the way. Looking over at T, she noticed that his upper body was moving, trying to drag his limp lower body away from the scene. She yelled at him, "Help will be here soon, stop trying to move or you might die!"

Officer Johnson had her hand on Officer Rodriguez's back and was asking him if he was okay. He still couldn't talk yet but nodded in response to her question. She then turned to me and asked, "How bad are you hurt?"

"Bad", it was all that I could manage to say. Suddenly, things started to spin, and my eyes rolled back into my head as the world around me came in and then went out of focus. I do remember hearing Officer Johnson yelling, "We need some help over here now!"

Although I was not aware of it at the time, Robyn was trying to reach me immediately after the shooting. Terry was holding her back, at first because he wasn't sure that I was even alive. When it became obvious that I was indeed still amongst the living, he did not want her to see me in such a sorry state. Terry was also well aware of our relationship; he knew if Robyn had made it to me that she would have never left my side. That would make for a very impossible situation with Tom, and Terry knew that would be the very last thing that I wanted to happen.

Terry looked her in the eyes and said, "I'm sorry, but you've got to get out of here, now! You know you can't be here."

"But…I need to help him…" Robyn stammered, wiping the tears from her eyes.

Trying to be as calm as possible, Terry said, "Look, there's nothing you can do for him now. I'll stay with him and call you when I know something."

"No! I'm not leaving him!" Robyn protested.

Chris and Lynn were now up and off the ground. Seeing Terry and Robyn, they made their way through the crowd. Trying to console Robyn, Lynn said, "He's going to be alright. The paramedics should be here any minute. There is nothing you can do for David now. You know that you have to leave before Tom finds out about this."

Terry, being the quick thinker that he is, told everyone, "Look, you all leave together, before the police start asking questions. I'll stay, and when the police ask me what happened, I'll say that just David and I were out celebrating his birthday, alone.

That way Robyn, you are never mentioned. You were with Chris and Lynn the whole time. Yes, you were downtown, but as far as anyone else is concerned you saw nothing. *Now go!"*

As Chris, and Lynn forcibly carried Robyn away, Robyn kept repeating, "Please don't die. Please don't die."

Terry walked up to the nearest Officer he saw and said, "Officer, Officer, I saw the whole fucking thing!"

As I drifted in and out of consciousness, I could distinctly hear Robyn's voice, audible above the chaos unfolding around me, saying over and over, 'Please don't die. Please don't die.'

Funny thing, Robyn's words were sharp and clear in my mind, yet I don't remember the EMTs arriving. I don't remember being placed on a gurney and wheeled to the nearest ambulance.

I don't remember the mad dash for the hospital, and I certainly don't remember the delicate, and lifesaving, surgery.

Are There Any Dead?

It was very early Sunday morning, in a place far removed from Orlando, when the telephone rang. Half asleep, a man answered the phone, "Hello?"

A familiar voice spoke, "Sir, there's been an incident in Orlando."

Trying to shake the sleep from his head, the mystery man asked, "What happened?"

The familiar voice said, "The details are sketchy, but there appears to have been a shoot-out of some sort."

Now fully awake, the mystery man continued to query his subordinate, "How many people were involved?"

The familiar voice replied, "Early reports indicate that there were at least six people involved."

Already knowing the answer, the mystery man asked, "Are there any dead?"

"At least two, maybe more," the response was steady and calm.

"And who was the shooter?" mystery man demanded.

The familiar voice replied, "Sir, everyone appears to have been armed. Who shot who, and why, has not been clarified yet—"

"Just what we need, a God damn shoot out with this bill pending in the House!" the mystery man snapped, "I want you to find out everything you can about those involved. Contact me again when you have more solid information about this fucking disaster!"

The familiar voice responded, "Yes sir."

Traci Kaneko entered the station a few minutes after this mysterious call had ended. Traci was an up-and-coming news reporter on the local network affiliate. The daughter of a Japanese professor and a Korean doctor, Traci had chosen a different path in life. With her thick, long black hair, and her trademark expressive eyes, Traci certainly had the looks for television; it was her knack for finding the story within a story that set her apart from the rest of the television hopefuls.

It was early Sunday morning, and she was in the office to begin coverage on the biggest local news event of the year. As she got to her desk, she noticed her message light was blinking. She picked up the receiver, dialed in her personal code, and heard the following message,

"*Hi Traci, this is Scott. I have a video of last night's shooting that you might be interested in. If so, call me on my cell, four-zero-seven…*"

She immediately called the number, and a gravelly voice said, "Hello?"

"Is this Scott?" Traci asked.

Annoyed with his sleep being disturbed, Scott answered, "Yeah, who's this?"

"This is Traci Kaneko…"

"Traci Kaneko, holy shit!", Scott proclaimed, "You're my favorite reporter. So, you want to see the video?"

Traci still wasn't sure if Scott was full of shit or not, but she had to give him the benefit of the doubt. She responded, "Yes, please email it to me."

Full of machismo, Scott said, "No, I'd like to show it to you in person."

Traci put the palm of her hand against her forehead, *Oh fuck, another obsessed fan!*

"Then can you bring it down to the station?" Traci asked.

"Yeah. Yeah, I can do that.", Scott said.

"How soon?"

"How about now?" Scott replied.

"Sure. When you get downstairs have the receptionist call me and I'll come down to meet you." Traci instructed.

"I'll see you soon," Scott replied.

Traci finished the conversation, "Okay, bye."

♦♦♦

Some thirty minutes later, true to his word, Scott showed up, and Traci went down to meet him.

"Oh my God, it's actually you, Traci. I'm such a huge fan," Scott gushed.

Without acknowledging his glee, Traci asked, "Can I please see the video?"

Pulling his phone out of his pocket, Scott said, "Yeah I have it here on my phone."

He proceeded to playback the video for Traci to watch.

When it was done, she asked, "Can you email me this?"

Scott asked, "Sure. Do you want me to go with you?"

Traci shook her head and said, "No, just stay here. I'll be back in a few moments after I get it."

The video clearly showed Officer Rodriguez as he drew his gun. A tall black man, who would later be positively identified as CJ, walked up behind Officer Rodriguez with his weapon drawn. There was a flash from CJ's gun, and then the unmistakable sound of 9mm discharging a round. The video looked as if the phone had been dropped, as the ensuing images were shaky and vague.

On the video, you could hear another shot, then another, and then multiple shots were fired. All the while, people were screaming in the background. When the camera finally came back into focus, the video showed a person on the ground, coming to rest on top of CJ and Officer Rodriguez.

The video ran for another minute, but you could see police officers arriving just before it cut off. However, the most interesting thing on the tape was a woman's voice, just off camera, repeating: *"Please don't die. Please don't die."*

The video shut off at that point. Traci said to herself, "I have a story to do!"

Traci returned to Scott and said, “Thank you very much for your video.”

Flush with confidence, Scott said, “You’re welcome. Tell me, would you like to go out sometime?”

“I’m sorry, but I have a boyfriend,” Traci lied.

♦♦♦

Within an hour, Traci had a story ready to go, complete with the only confirmed video to exist that started before the first shot was fired. The story ran that Sunday morning, at noon, and then again at the six and eleven broadcasts. Although the names and ages of the persons involved had not yet been released by the authorities, it was clear that a racial component would certainly become a part of the story. However, what part would be determined by the court of public opinion.

We Will Continue with Our Story After A Brief Intermission.

I was unconscious during the next three days, but a lot happened during my absence. On Sunday, the *incident* was the story of the day. All the local networks were trying to outdo one another with an exclusive this, and an exclusive that. Each station was trying desperately to interview anyone who was present, not present, or even remotely involved with any of the participants.

By Monday, the story had been picked up and reported at the national level by all of the dedicated cable news networks. By Tuesday morning, the story went primetime - national, airing on all the network morning shows. The coverage was mostly rehashed local network stuff, but here is what the public, and others, did find out:

THE DEAD:

Calvin Jones, aka "CJ", 22. A long list of felony charges including: armed robbery, assault, narcotics possession, attempted murder, and grand theft auto. Additionally, ballistics tests on the 9 mm handgun used by Calvin connected the weapon to a double homicide 18 months prior. Calvin should have been in jail at the time of the shooting; however, he was released two weeks earlier, after receiving time off for good behavior.

Curtis Jones, aka "Little CJ", 17; Curtis was the younger brother of Calvin Jones. Curtis had no prior criminal record and was unarmed.

William Baker, aka "Willie B", 24. He also had a very long list of felony convictions, including manslaughter. At the time of the shooting, William had an outstanding arrest warrant for parole violation. Additionally, ballistics tests matched William's weapon to an unsolved bank robbery 2 months earlier. William left behind an ex-wife and a 2-year-old son.

Marcus Porter, aka "Tiny", 20, was a person of interest in a home invasion that resulted in the death of one woman. Ballistics tests confirmed his weapon was indeed the murder weapon. The authorities also considered Tiny to be a mid-level drug dealer and a suspect in several unsolved armed robberies.

THE WOUNDED:

Theo Roberts, aka "T", 21, had a criminal record that included possession of drug paraphernalia, resisting arrest without violence, and trespassing. Ballistics tests did not connect his weapon to any prior crime. However, the gun had been reported stolen some two years earlier in Atlanta. In addition, Theo's wounds had left him paralyzed from the waist down.

David Alan Taylor, 30, a Telecommunications Sales Manager with no criminal history. Wounds were quite extensive, including gunshot wounds to the left thigh, right shoulder, and chest. Currently listed in critical condition.

Diane Walters, 38, a Business Analyst married to Jack Walters, a successful local construction company owner. Diane's injuries were considered minor; she received a broken nose and a chipped tooth. Treated and released.

Craig Davis, 24, a coworker of Diane Walters, his wounds were much more serious. Craig had a broken nose, broken jaw, four broken ribs, internal injuries, and lost five teeth. Currently listed in stable condition and expected to make a full recovery.

Peter Watson, 27. A construction worker, Peter thought it would be a great idea to jump up on a planter to see what was happening. Turns out he was shot in the stomach by an errant shot. Currently listed in stable condition.

THE ORLANDO POLICE DEPARTMENT (OPD) PARTICIPANTS:

Officer Mike Thomas, 32. Mike was a 10-year veteran with an exceptional law enforcement record, receiving multiple citations and awards for service.

Officer Paul Rodriguez, 27. Paul had been with the Orlando Police Department for two years. Previously Officer Rodriguez served six years in the Army. He is married and a father of three, two boys and one girl.

Officer Debra Johnson, 37. Married with one boy, Debra had been with the department for twelve years.

Officer Doug Johnson, 42. Doug had been with the department for seven years. Prior to working for the Orlando Police Department, Officer Johnson was a police officer for the nearby city of Sanford.

There were also many witnesses of the downtown shooting; each with their own story to tell, and to whomever would listen. A number of additional OPD officers and other first responders, including Firefighters and Paramedics, were interviewed with great frequency. Eventually, even the Mayor and Police Chief got involved.

As usual, to get the story out first, there were a lot of, how should I say, 'less than actual facts' reported. These faulty facts included the locations of the events, the number of people injured or dead, the timeline, and order of events; as well as the ages, ethnic backgrounds, and occupations of those involved. But I think some of the most interesting coverage came from the print media. It wasn't what they were reporting that I would find fascinating; it was the headlines they used. My personal favorite that I heard about later was: *Shoot out at the Mouse Corral!*

By Tuesday morning, the news coverage had the basic facts right. All the major networks were now reporting that, in a parking garage a few blocks away from the *incident*, two people were robbed, separately, at gunpoint. Within a few minutes after the robberies were reported, an alert police officer, Paul Rodriguez, spotted the alleged perpetrators and followed them from a safe distance down Church Street.

Within moments, Officer Rodriguez decided that it was in the best interest of civilian safety to call in backup before confronting the alleged perpetrators. At that time, another gang member pulled a weapon and shot Officer Rodriguez in the back. His bulletproof vest was credited with initially saving his life.

Additionally, it was then generally agreed that a Good Samaritan saved Officer Rodriguez from being shot in the head when a bystander picked up the officer's weapon and shot all five alleged suspects prior to police backup arriving. In the process, the bystander had been shot multiple times and required immediate medical attention.

Meanwhile, four of the alleged suspects died, and the fifth was paralyzed from the waist down. It certainly was a very compelling story with what appeared to be a Good Samaritan coming to the aid of a stricken law enforcement officer, culminating in a happy ending for truth, justice, and the American way.

Case closed, right?

Well, not exactly.

♦♦♦

Investigators were becoming very suspicious; the eyewitness accounts were not consistent with the evidence being discovered at the crime scene.

Diane was still sticking with her story about being robbed on the ground floor of the parking garage, and then finding Craig on the third floor, beaten, and left for dead. However, a preliminary search turned up Diane's stolen purse in the stairwell, between the second and third floors of the parking garage. Also, Craig's car was still parked at home, but Diane's car was parked on the third floor of the parking garage. And, finally, Diane's blood type was found on the wall next to the elevator. There was no blood on the ground floor where she claimed the robbery had occurred. Craig was no help because he claimed not to remember anything before, during, or after the attack.

The Truth Shall Set You Free

By Sunday morning, the police investigation was well under way. Due to the usual office politics bullshit, Detective Chris Welles had been assigned as the lead detective for both crime scenes. Detective Derek Miller, a tall man with wavy blonde hair, had been given the responsibility of conducting interrogations by Welles.

Miller hated playing second banana to anyone in the Department, but he especially detested working under Welles. With more time on the force, and more time investigating high profile crimes, Detective Miller felt that the case should have been handed to him on a silver platter. Instead, he was stuck in that fucking interrogation room while Welles posed for the cameras.

Those close to the investigation, especially Derek Miller, were becoming very suspicious. Detective Miller knew deep in his gut that Diane was lying, but he didn't know why. So,

Detective Miller had Diane brought in for a more thorough interrogation.

Diane looked nervous as she was led into the interrogation room, where she waited for several minutes before being joined by Detective Miller and his partner Ryan Baker. Detective Baker was one of the youngest detectives in the police department, and he looked the part. Baker had reddish hair and a boyish face that he tried to hide behind a beard, but everyone still referred to him as Opie, a reference to his obvious resemblance to the role made famous by Ron Howard.

Baker had been a Detective for only six months now and was the real reason why Detective Miller had not been made lead investigator. Knowing this and coupled with the fact that he still felt uncomfortable in the interrogation room, Detective Baker decided to keep a very low profile on this investigation.

Miller, on the other hand, was an old school cop; he loved interrogations. To him, it was like playing a game of chess, *for real*. Frequently, the paperwork and office politics made Miller question this profession, but it was the thrill of the chase that kept him in the game.

Over the years, Detective Miller had developed a talent for spotting and exploiting the weakness of his opponents. He could tell within seconds if his opponent would talk, or not. He would spend hours toying with his opponents and wasn't afraid to bend the rules when needed. After all, there is the way things should be, and then there is the way that produced results.

That day was different however; Welles, had seen to that. Just minutes before entering the interrogation room, Detective Miller had watched Detective Welles issue a statement on the local news. Noticeably absent from Welles speech, was the acknowledgement of Miller's involvement. This turned a normally surly Detective Miller into a raging monster.

Today, Detective Miller would not be a chess master, he had a personal agenda: solve this fucking thing quick, and then put that asshole, Welles in his place. One look at Diane, and Detective Miller knew that she would, eventually, tell him everything.

Detective Baker spoke first, "Diane, can we get you anything? A coffee or a soda?"

After several seconds, a shaking Diane replied, "No."

Detectives Miller and Baker then sat down across from Diane. Already positioned in the middle of the table, a tape recorder patiently waited for the interview to begin. Miller hit the record button and made the usual remarks, noting the date, the time, and the participants of the interview before beginning his interrogation.

"Diane," he said, "I know you are lying about what happened, but what troubles me is why."

"No…. I told you everything, like it happened," Diane tried to sound convincing.

"No, you did not!" Detective Miller bellowed.

Diane lowered her head but said nothing. One of the tricks in Detective Miller's arsenal was the outright fabrication of the truth. Miller knew that, with an outrageous lie, he could spook a timid person into talking, and Diane looked very timid today.

He stated, "You know what I think? I think that you planned this whole thing!"

"No… I…No I did not," Diane stammered.

He had Diane now, so he mixed in a little truth to confuse her even more, "Then why did we find your purse in the stairwell?"

Diane replied, "I don't know."

Now it was time to set the hook, Detective Miller countered, "Then why was your car parked on the third floor, and Craig's car was at home?"

Diane continued to look down at the ground, but still said nothing. The rage was now oozing out of every pore of Miller's body, “Look, I know you picked up Craig and brought him to the parking garage, so those monsters could kill him!”

“No… I… wouldn’t,” Diane cried.

Detective Miller slammed his fist on the table, annoyed by Diane's denial, “Yes, you did!”

“No…I.”, Diane stammered.

“You what?” Detective Miller demanded, “You wanted to have Craig killed, admit it!”

Diane, looking up from the floor, defiantly shouted, “No!”

“Then tell us the fucking truth!” he shouted back.

With tears now rolling down her face, Diane said, “I want a lawyer.”

Detective Miller expected this response at some point. They *all* ask for a lawyer, but he wasn’t giving up on this confession.

“I’ll charge you with murder if you bring a lawyer into this now!”

“What?” Diane asked.

“In the state of Florida, if a person is killed during the commission of a crime, then *any* person involved in the crime can be charged with murder. You are guilty of wanting Craig killed, and you are also guilty of what happened after the fact!"

"No!" Diane protested, "I want a lawyer!"

Detective Miller reached over and hit the pause button before responding,

"You're not getting a fucking lawyer. Now tell me the truth."

Detective Baker reached over and grabbed the arm of Miller. Baker leaned in and whispered, "We need to stop. She asked for a lawyer."

Miller pulled away and shouted, "Tell me the fucking truth now! Or so help me God, I'm gonna make sure you end up on death row!"

"Please.... I can't," Diane begged.

"Then tell me the fucking truth about what happened.", Detective Miller demanded, "I can't help you if you don't tell me the truth."

Diane cried for several minutes. Miller knew that he had her on the verge of breaking, so he switched gears. In a calm, gentle tone he said, "Diane, I want to help you. I don't think that you meant for all this to happen, so just tell me the truth. I promise that whatever you say will not leave this room."

Diane looked up, "You promise?"

Detective Miller lied, "Yeah, I promise."

Crying, Diane could no longer contain her guilt,

"I didn't try to kill Craig; I love him. We were at a bar, and we just came across those guys as we went back to my car.

"We were attacked on the third floor, and they hurt Craig so bad… I said I was on the ground floor because… I tried to cover it up because I didn't want Jack to know about our affair."

An extremely pleased Detective Miller sighed, "Thank you for your honesty. You are free to go."

"You won't tell anyone what I've said?" Diane asked.

"No, your secret is safe with us," Detective Miller said.

The investigators thanked her for her honesty and assured her that there would be no mention of the affair in the official records. Of course, the very next day, an unnamed source leaked the details of the investigation, including the affair, to the local news media.

Later that evening they found Diane in her parked car at a local park. At some point, after seeing the exclusive report detailing her affair with Craig, she took one of Jack's handguns, drove to the park, and blew her brains out. A neatly folded note was found on the passenger seat.

It said:

Jack,

I am so sorry. I didn't mean for this to happen. I never stopped loving you, but I just couldn't help myself. It was a foolish thing to do, but now I just don't see any other way out of this situation. Please remember that I loved you, and someday, I hope to see you again.

Diane

♦♦♦

Within hours of Diane's suicide, the media began to swarm around the house, hoping to catch a glimpse of the devastated husband, Jack. The media would get far more than they ever bargained for.

Jack sat alone in the darkness of the house, drinking his Scotch straight from the bottle. There before him on the coffee table, were various pictures of the two of them during happier times. Apparently, Diane had looked at the pictures one last time before she fled the safety of the house and then killed herself.

In between swigs, Jack sifted thru the pictures, only pausing to pick up the occasional snapshot and reminisce about what he had lost that day. He wanted to cry, but, for some reason, the tears just would not fall. Meanwhile, the lights of the media outside made their presence felt by casting odd shadows on the walls.

Sometime around nine, Jack succumbed to the despair that he felt. He stumbled into the bedroom, unlocked his gun safe, and he reached inside. Pulling out a 9mm handgun, he carefully loaded the gun and sat down on the edge of bed. Falling back, Jack held the gun up in the air and considered what he should do next.

After chambering a round, Jack closed his eyes, and finally wept.

Several minutes later, Jack sat up, took one last swig of Scotch, and then headed for the front door. Pausing at the door, he looked out the window and saw several news vans parked across the street. He closed his eyes and counted to ten before throwing back the deadbolt latch and opening the door. As the door swung open, countless news cameras aimed their lights in his direction.

On cue, Jack stepped out the door, and started shouting, "This is all your fault! You fucking did this to her!"

Jack pulled the gun from behind his back and started firing at the crowd. Screams erupted as the bullets peppered the news vans. Jack continued pulling the trigger, fifteen rounds in all, until the gun was empty. He then walked back inside his house and closed the door.

Somewhere in the distance, sirens began to wail.

A couple of minutes later, one last shot was heard.

I Don't Remember...

It was the next day and Terry still was not changing his story about the two of us being out alone, celebrating my birthday. The police now had eyewitness testimony from customers, and employees claiming that we were hanging out with at least two other people. The police also had additional eyewitness testimony that identified three people, a man and two women, talking with Terry at the scene of the shooting. The three then fled the scene before the perimeter could be secured.

Detective Miller had been devastated by the suicide of Diane. In his rush to embarrass Welles, Miller had forgotten to consider how Diane would react to the publicity surrounding her affair. For the first time in his life, he was questioning his own judgment. However, there was still a job to do, and years of police training told him that Terry was covering up something. The only way to right this moment of foolish pride was to close this case, so Detective Miller had Terry brought down to the station for additional questioning.

Terry was led into a room where he sat for nearly thirty minutes before being joined by Detectives Miller and Baker. Like countless times before, Miller sized up his opponent, and immediately decided that Terry would not be talking today.

The interrogation began quite cordially with Detective Baker saying, "Terry, thank you for coming in today—"

Terry interrupted, "Like I had a choice."

"No, you didn't," retorted Detective Miller. "So, let's cut the bullshit and you tell me what really happened."

Terry replied, "Like I said before, David and I were out celebrating his birthday—"

"With who?" Miller demanded.

"Just the two of us," Terry replied.

"Bullshit. I'll ask one more time, with who?" Miller fired back.

"Just the two of us," Terry responded again.

Miller picked up his notepad and shook it in Terry's face; "I have several eyewitnesses that place at least two other people with you at the bar."

"Like I said before, it was just the two of us," Terry replied, "We had a couple of drinks with some strangers, but that's it."

Trying to rattle Terry's confidence, Detective Miller asked an unexpected question, "Are you two a couple?"

Surprised by the question, Terry asked, "What?"

Miller smirked, "Are you two a couple? I mean, are you gay or something?"

Terry laughed, "No."

"It seems really odd to me that the two of you went out, *by yourselves*," Detective Miller stressed.

Terry asked, "So what?"

"Are you a fag?" Miller quipped, "Do you like to suck dicks?"

Terry laughed again, "Fuck you."

"That's original," Miller said.

Pushing buttons and asking uncomfortable questions were just a part of Miller's tactics. It's not like he believed what he would posit, he just used it to elicit a visceral response. Angry people make more mistakes, and Miller was quickly running out of opportunities to wrest the truth from Terry.

Terry demanded, “I want a lawyer.”

“Fuck the lawyer, tell me the truth.” Detective Miller roared, “Who were you with that night?”

Terry stared defiantly into Miller’s eyes, and repeated, “I want a lawyer.”

“Who else was with you?” Detective Miller shouted.

Terry said nothing.

Unwilling to let this civilian off so easily, Detective Miller said, “Answer me, or I’ll make your life miserable.”

Terry still said nothing.

Detective Miller demanded, “Answer me, or I’ll execute a search warrant on your house.”

“On what grounds?” Terry asked.

Detective Miller smiled, “Probable cause.”

Terry sneered, “What probable cause?”

Detective Miller answered, “I think that you might be a drug dealer.”

It was standard procedure to seek a search warrant based upon ‘probable cause’. What exactly that meant was left up to the judge. Yes, it was always easy enough to get a search warrant for drugs, but Miller had no intention of pursuing this course of action. He was hoping that just the threat would be enough to break Terry; it wasn't.

Terry laughed, "Yeah, you wish."

"I'll tear your house apart looking for drugs, and there is nothing you can do about it…smart ass."

"I want a lawyer." Terry demanded.

"And I want the truth. Who else were you with?" Miller insisted.

Terry asked, "Am I being charged with a crime at this time?"

"No," Detective Baker said.

"Not yet," Detective Miller added, "But if you do not start cooperating with us, I will charge you with obstruction of justice."

"Then charge me and get me a lawyer or let me go," Terry replied.

"I don't think you understand the gravity of this situation," Detective Miller said, "I have four dead people, and another one paralyzed from the waist down. There is no doubt that your friend did this, and the sooner you tell us what really happened, the sooner we can close this case and move on with our lives."

Terry emphatically stated, “I have nothing more to say.”

Detective Miller moved within inches of Terry’s face, close enough to kiss.

“This is your last chance Terry to tell me the truth. If you walk out those doors and I find out later that you have left out *any* detail, then I will have you arrested.”

Terry asked, “Anything else?”

“Have a nice fucking day,” Detective Miller snorted.

After Terry walked out of the room, Detective Baker said, “Way to go Miller.”

Detective Miller replied, “Fuck you, Opie.”

Meanwhile in another part of town…

The Metamorphosis of Theo Roberts

Even before Theo Roberts had opened his eyes, he knew exactly where he was in this dangerous world. He had always known where he was, but he just wanted to—somehow—break free from the trappings of this place. Yes, Theo was destined for more than life had given him; yet here he was, once again, a victim of fate.

The familiar sound of a heart monitor echoed through the hospital room, each beat breaking his heart into smaller and smaller pieces. Those memories, the ones that he had tried so hard to forget, now came flooding back into his mind. He tried to focus on the pain, but it was no use; the telltale beat of the monitor kept bringing him back to that awful day. It was the same horrid noise that he had heard as he stood there by his mother's bed, waiting for her to die. Finally, Theo shouted in his mind.

Open your fucking eyes!

He looked around the room. Spartan by design, this place was sterile and devoid of the life that he had craved for so many years. He tried to lift his hand to wipe the sleep away from his eyes, but it pulled tight and stopped. Looking down, Theo could see that he was shackled to the bed. He tried to sit up but found that he couldn't move. Terrified, he laid there trapped as the steady beat of the heart monitor pushed him further and further into the darkest recesses of his mind.

Now that he was awake, Detectives could question him about his involvement in the events of Saturday night. Without ever meeting Theo, Detective Miller sized up his next opponent. Theo was familiar with the legal system, and no regular interrogation would make him talk. Theo would act tough and pretend to be proud, but Detective Miller knew that, sooner or later, Theo would ask for a deal. Theo's type *always* wanted a deal, so Detective Miller decided to have a little fun first.

"Theo, what happened Saturday night?" Miller asked.

Theo replied, "I don't remember."

"Come on Theo, you know what happened," Miller countered.

Theo responded, "No, I can't remember a fucking thing."

Miller closed his eyes tightly, and rubbed his temples with the tips of his fingers for a couple of minutes before continuing, "Theo, so how does it feel to be a cripple?"

"Fuck you!" Theo lashed out.

Looking over to Baker, Miller smiled, "Sensitive, isn't he?"

Baker said nothing; instead, he took his right hand and pulled it down his face while closing his eyes. He had wanted to crawl under a rock and hide. Determined not to add anything to this conversation, Detective Baker remained silent.

Detective Miller returned his attention to the now agitated Theo Roberts, and asked again, "So how does it feel to be a crippled nigger?"

"Fuck you!" Theo, once again, shouted.

Unfazed by Theo's hostility, he continued, "Are you so full of nigger pride that you would let some white boy get away with shooting you?"

Theo shook his head and laughed under his breath, but he said nothing.

"Theo, why were you and the others at the parking garage?" Detective Miller asked.

Theo replied, "I don't remember being there."

Detective Miller pushed, “Why did you beat that poor kid nearly to death?”

“I don’t remember doing that.” Theo responded.

Detective Miller was losing what little patience he had, “What happened when you reached Church Street?”

“I don’t remember being there.” Theo protested.

The detective sarcastically asked, “I suppose you don’t remember the shooting?”

Theo answered, “No, I don’t.”

Detective Miller asked, “Can you explain to me why you got shot?”

Theo smiled.

“I don’t know. Maybe this guy shot me…. because I’m black.”

Detective Miller chuckled, “Really? Are you sure that this guy killing your friends had nothing to do with it?”

“I think that I was just minding my own business.” Theo answered.

“Yeah, I bet.” Detective Miller snorted.

Theo continued, “I was just an innocent bystander. I didn’t do anything.”

Detective Miller asked, “So what about all those eyewitnesses that saw you shoot this guy?”

“They must be mistaken. I mean, don’t we all look alike to you white folk?” Theo retorted.

“Stop wasting my time,” Detective Miller said, “or I’ll see that you spend the rest of your life in jail.”

Theo surprised Miller by finally getting to the point so quickly, “I want a deal first. I want immunity. For *everything*.”

Detective Miller smiled, “We can work something out, just tell me what happened…”

Theo interrupted, “Put it in writing.”

Miller replied, “Sure, but first, tell me what happened…”

Theo demanded, “Put the deal in writing, and then I’ll talk.”

The first thing Detective Miller did after leaving the hospital was to call Welles. After a couple rings, Welles answered.

“This is Welles.”

Lighting up a cigarette, Detective Miller said, “Welles, it’s Miller.”

Welles asked, “How did it go with Roberts?”

"He wants a deal," Detective Miller responded.

"Of course, he does," Welles scoffed.

Miller shot back, "Not just any deal, he wants immunity for everything, including that home invasion. And he wants it all in writing."

Welles laughed.

"Alright, just for fun I'll run it by the D.A."

Already annoyed with Welles, Miller responded, "Yeah, you do that."

Detective Miller hung up the phone, crushed out his cigarette, and mumbled under his breath— "Asshole."

♦♦♦

Theo had nothing but time to think about why the sound of a heart monitor terrified him. A memory, long suppressed, made its way back to the surface of Theo's mind. It had been nearly three years now, since his mother had passed. The last words she spoke crashed through his broken soul.

"Son, make something of your life. Promise me, you'll make something of your life."

"Yes, mama. I promise. Please don't die. Please don't leave me here alone..." Theo begged her at the time.

In desperation, Theo looked up to Heaven and asked God to help his mother. It was hard to know if God had answered his prayer or not, but tears streamed down Theo's face as the beat faltered, only to give way to one long, sad tone.

Ever since that dreadful day, Theo had plotted his escape from this place. And every scheme, plan, and idea he ever had would be derailed by Life's little complexities. In that neighborhood, life was a struggle, a losing battle between boredom and frustration. Boredom led to drugs and alcohol abuse; frustration led to violence.

Ever since being admitted to the hospital, Theo Roberts had received just a handful of visitors. Most were friends and family, but one person stood out above the rest. Richard Bishop, the hospital chaplain, had stopped by to talk to Theo. Although a slight man with wire-rimmed glasses and a receding hairline, Richard possessed a tenacity that Theo had never seen before. At first, Theo ignored Richard, hoping the religious hired gun would just give up, but, unbeknownst to him, Richard never gave up on a challenge.

Richard would come by and talk to Theo about the glory of God and the power of faith; Theo would just watch the television. After a while, though, Theo would catch himself listening to Richard. It was the passion that Richard exuded, a belief so powerful that Theo could not help but to notice.

Finally, Theo spoke to Richard.

"You do realize that I am paralyzed."

Richard replied, "Yes, my son, but you are still alive."

Theo asked, "Why? I can't use my legs; I might as well be dead."

Richard responded, "The Lord still had plans for you."

"What can I do? I am just half a man now," Theo requested.

Richard smiled, "Your legs may longer work, but your heart, and your mind, are still at your disposal."

Theo laughed, "What good are they?"

Richard replied, "That is something that you must decide for yourself. But trust in the Lord, and *He* shall show you the way."

Theo asked, "Do you know what I've done?"

Richard stated, "It doesn't matter to the Lord, but yes, I do. I have seen it on the news."

Theo continued, "Did you know that the DA could cut me a deal? I may be absolved from my crimes. I could now be a free man—"

"But you still seem troubled my son," Richard interjected.

Surprised by the insight of a frail man, Theo answered—"Yes. I would have thought I would feel better by now. But for some reason, I still feel kinda hollow inside."

Richard smiled, "That's because you have not made peace with the Lord. Once you accept the Lord as your savior, then you will feel the peace that you so desperately long for."

Theo immediately dismissed the notion of the Lord's forgiveness, but over the next couple of days, Theo began to slowly realize that God *was* calling him. In the presence of Richard Bishop, Theo would finally accept Jesus as his savior, and take the first initial steps toward the man that he would soon become. In the sterile environment of the hospital, Theo devoured the lessons of The Bible and sought the enlightenment of the ages.

It occurred to Theo that friends like CJ, Willie B, Little CJ, and Tiny had helped ease the pain, if only for a short while, but Theo had always liked to be alone with his thoughts. Sometimes, he would aimlessly wander around the neighborhood. Often, for no apparent reason, he would find himself standing on the steps of the church.

It would be more than two years of this pilgrimage before Theo could bring himself to enter the sanctuary. Once inside, he would take a seat in the back pew and talk to his mother. Sometimes, he found himself talking to God as well. It was during one of these sessions, early afternoon on a Saturday in November, that Theo had asked God for a sign.

"Please give me something, some kind of sign, so I can honor Mama's last request. Please, God, get me out of this life. I need to get out of this life."

The realization that his prayer had actually been answered, just not in the manner that Theo had recognized, was the catalyst necessary to propel him toward the light. At some point, in the middle of a moonlit night, Theo had a vision. Theo would reach out to the community that needed guidance. Theo would open a community center for children of all ages to attend, a place where everyone could feel safe. As promised by Richard Bishop, the Lord had finally shown the way, and Theo Roberts was determined to spread the joy.

Theo listened in silence as the Doctor, once again, explained the true extent of his injuries. This time, Theo was filled with love and forgiveness. The medical term was paraplegic, but Theo, well he felt free as a bird soaring high above the jungle. Though he would never walk again, God had indeed given Theo a sign, and he could now rise above this place.

Theo smiled as the man he once was faded away, and there, in its place, a new man sprang to life. One filled with joy and blessed with a purpose. One finally at peace with the universe and the so-called limitations of the body and soul. The mind and heart were now free, nothing else mattered, and, in a unique way, he was right. For that man, who did those terrible things, no longer existed.

That man was gone, never to return.

In This Corner We Have Our Local Hero & All-Around Good Guy

It was 3:12 PM on a Tuesday that I finally opened my eyes. I remember thinking to myself, *Shit! It's not a dream.*

The sounds of very expensive medical equipment, monitoring God knows what, permeated the small private room that I was in. I had tubes and wires all over me, and my head hurt like hell, but hey, I was still alive. But how alive was the big question weighing on my mind. Did I lose any of my cognitive skills, would I walk again, could I speak again?

I didn't have wait too long; a nurse came into the room. She must have read the expression on my face, and before I could even attempt to say anything, she spoke with such a sweet voice.

"Hello. You had us really worried for a while there, but it looks like you're going to be okay. There are some people here who would like to see you. I'll send them in just as soon as the doctor talks to you. Please don't try to talk; you have some tubes in you that will prevent you from speaking. Do you understand?"

I slightly nodded my head and just waited for the doctor. Twenty minutes later, the doctor came in. He spent a few minutes flipping through my chart; it looked to me more like he was just stalling for time, trying to come up with the right choice of words.

He then began to speak, "Mr. Taylor, you suffered some very serious injuries Saturday night. The gunshot to your shoulder was superficial, but the remaining two gunshot wounds were a source of much greater concern to us. The shot to your left thigh fractured your femur. It caused extensive damage to the muscles and soft tissue surrounding your femur. This injury will require a great deal of rehabilitation.

"The shot to your chest, however, was life threatening; bullet fragments have lodged in behind your heart. We had to perform a very delicate operation to remove them. You were very lucky, Mr. Taylor; a few centimeters to the left and you would not have survived."

I nodded, acknowledging what the doctor had said, and I gestured that I wanted my tubes removed so that I could talk.

He nodded and said, "Since you are awake, we will see if we can remove the tubes now."

♦♦♦

Now that I had regained consciousness, the police wanted to speak with me. So, I spent most of Tuesday night talking with Detective Chris Welles, the lead detective on the parking garage and related shooting crime scenes. A very short, stout, balding man with curly black hair and glasses, Detective Welles made me feel very comfortable and listened intently to my recollection of the event.

I gave him all the details that I could remember from the actual shooting, but I was less than specific when it came to who I was with prior to the shooting. It was my intention to protect Robyn's involvement, so I told Detective Welles that I remember being at the bar with Terry, we met some people, had a few drinks, and that was it.

Welles told me that many eyewitnesses had heard a woman pleading for me not to die, and he wanted to know if I knew who this mystery woman was. I explained that, yes, I did hear someone say something to that effect, but I did not know who she was. After some time, he thanked me for my cooperation and left me to be alone with my family.

Now when the nurse said a few people were waiting to talk to me, I thought she meant some family and friends. What she really meant to say was that every single major network in the United States (and even some from as far away as Japan) had at least one reporter waiting outside the hospital to talk to me, my family, or anyone else that had seen me. The world was, impatiently, waiting to hear what I had to say.

A press conference was set up for Thursday morning at 9 AM. To begin the conference, my doctor first described my medical condition, the surgeries that I had endured, and the future rehabilitation that I would require. He then fielded a few questions, and without further ado, I was wheeled out and up to the microphone. I remember seeing nothing but lights and flashes, hearing the din of a hundred people, trying to ask me something different, all at the same time.

I was thinking to myself: *Why are all these people here?*

I still didn't understand how this became an international media event. I nervously answered the usual set of questions:

"How do you feel?"

"Do you think you're a hero?"

"Would you do it again?"

"Why did you do it?"

Only one question throughout the whole session caught my attention; it was posed by Traci Kaneko, a local TV reporter.

"What do you think of the current gun control laws, and do you think the pending gun control legislation might have prevented this tragedy?"

It was a relevant question, and one that I felt deserved a well thought out response. Unfortunately, I didn't have one. To compound matters, I didn't take the time to carefully choose my words.

After a brief pause, I began to speak, "I don't think the current gun laws go far enough. I would like to see an eventual reduction and additional restrictions on the production of assault rifles and handguns, in particular. I assume it was the easy availability of handguns that made this whole situation possible."

I took a deep breath before I continued, "I am not looking to ban all guns. On the contrary, I feel it is a right that law abiding citizens should be allowed to possess firearms. Still, I think there are too many loopholes in the enforcement of the current gun laws, that allow guns to be illegally purchased, or traded, without proper background checks to ensure these deadly weapons do not end up in the hands of felons."

It sounded great in my head; however, it turned out to be a declaration of war, only I didn't know it at the time. I went on to field a few more questions, and after another ten minutes or so, I asked my doctor to remove me. I was beginning to tire, and the pressure of the press conference was just too much for me. I apologized to the media and said I would answer more questions when I felt better.

♦♦♦

Shortly after my first press conference ended, the phone rang again in that same place far removed from Orlando. Again, the same man answered in a gravelly voice, "Hello?"

"Sir, we have a problem." the concern was evident in the familiar voice.

Unsure of what to expect, the mystery man asked, "What is it?"

"Listen to this sir," the caller played back part of my press conference, only the part regarding the gun control question and my rambling answer. When the playback was done, he asked, "Sir, what should we do?"

With his anger rising by the second, the mystery man said, "Bury the fuck! Find out all the dirt you can on this cock sucker and forward it to someone in the press!"

The caller asked, "Who, sir?"

Annoyed, the mystery man said, "What about what's her name, the one who ran that piece on us last year?"

The caller replied, “Rhonda Spears, sir.”

“Yes, Rhonda Spears. Filter everything you find out through her, I want you to dig up every little secret from his pathetic life, and I want her to use it to destroy any support he might get from the general public. We can’t afford to have any type of sympathy for this asshole!

“Then I want you to contact our friends in the House and Senate, remind them of our contributions in the past. Explain to them why it would be in their best interest to distance themselves from this so-called Good Samaritan.

“Do you understand?”

“Yes sir,” the familiar voice replied.

Suddenly the phone went dead. The familiar voice didn’t have time to be offended; he had work to do.

♦♦♦

Rhonda Spears had been a network reporter at a national network for some time now, however, she had not managed to elevate herself above the others vying for airtime. With blonde hair and blue eyes, Rhonda may have looked like an angel; but her drive to succeed forged a working relationship with the Devil. She was sitting at her desk when the call came in.

A familiar voice asked, “Rhonda?”

“Yes,” Rhonda answered.

The caller asked, “Do you know who this is?”

Again, Rhonda answered, “Yes.”

“Could you use some interesting and colorful information on this David Taylor? You know, the one involved in that shooting in Orlando.”

Ripe with curiosity, Rhonda asked, “What do you have?”

The familiar voice continued, “Many things.”

Rhonda was just short of begging now, “Like what?”

“I’ll send you the file. Understand; we want you to use this information to discredit him. We want to be sure that the general public has no sympathy for him, or anything that he might say.”

Trying to feign indifference, Rhonda asked, “Why should I?”

“Think of this as an investment in your future,” the familiar voice advised. “Think of this as an opportunity to shape the future of your country.”

There was a pause, long enough for the air to grow thick and heavy.

“Think of this as a threat to expose your own dirty little secrets.

“Do we have an understanding?”

Rhonda swallowed, “Yes, we do.”

Enter Dr. James Johnson

Born in Harlem, Jesse James Johnson, was named after his paternal grandfather, Jesse Johnson, and his maternal grandfather, James Freeman. These two men would play an essential role in the life of JJ, as they liked to call him. One from Mississippi, and the other from Alabama, both men grew up under the specter of Jim Crow laws and, firsthand, had experienced the cruelty of unabashed racism.

At a young age, both men would escape the oppression of the South and seek the opportunities of New York City. Once there, each man married, had children, and prospered in this new environment. Living only blocks from each other for many years, these men had never met each other until their children began dating. When JJ was born, these men developed a special relationship with their first grandchild.

Though far removed from the South, their voices still hinted at their humble origins. As a child, JJ was fascinated by this strange combination of New York harshness, mixed with that unmistakable Southern drawl. He practiced and practiced until he, too, could enunciate in the same cadence.

But Jesse Johnson and James Freeman imparted something more on JJ than just a unique speech pattern, they passed on their anger directed at whites. They told JJ about the beatings they had survived, the lawmen who would always look the other way, and the threat of death that came with every sunset. They talked about family who had been lynched, friends unfairly imprisoned, and the hopelessness wrought by the indifference of whites to the daily injustices of black life in the South. Never trust a white man, they would always say, and JJ would learn this lesson the hard way.

When JJ was thirteen, he and some friends ventured to Midtown. As they walked the streets, he could feel the eyes of the world upon him and his friends. As they passed a grocery stand, he accidently bumped the table and an apple fell to the ground. He bent over and picked it up, ready to place the apple back on the pile, when the owner yelled, “Stop! Thief!”

JJ never saw the cop arrive on the scene; the man was there so quick it was if he had materialized from thin air. The cop asked. “What’s the matter, Bob?”

"This nigger-boy was trying to steal an apple!" The owner sneered.

The cop asked, "Is that true, boy? Were you stealing an apple?"

Terrified, the thoughts of his grandfathers' words pulsated in his mind, JJ stammered, "N-no sir, I bumped the table and the apple just fell. I-I-I was trying to put it back."

The owner countered, "The nigger touched it, I can't sell that apple now."

The cop looked down at JJ and his friends, "Do any of you have any money?"

JJ and his friends nodded, each pulled out some change from their pockets, and held it out for the cop to see. The cop grabbed all the money, handed the owner some change, and then put the rest in his pocket. "You boys had better get back to your own neighborhood."

With no money left, he and his friends had to walk all the way back to Harlem. It was a hard lesson he had learned, and one that he would never forget. As the years passed, JJ first lost Grandpa Jesse, and then Grandpa James too, but the lessons they taught JJ, and the stories they told, stayed forever in his heart.

When it was time, JJ went off to college. Not just any college, but the prestigious Emory College in Atlanta. It was there, in Atlanta, that he first heard of Dr. Martin Luther King, Jr. and the thunderous sermons delivered in the cause of civil rights. JJ would travel to participate in marches, sit-ins, and other events pursuing equal rights for blacks. And, like many in America, he openly wept when Dr. King was assassinated.

It was in his grief that JJ founded what would eventually become the African Americans Laboring Against Racial Misconduct, or A.L.A.R.M; an organization dedicated to the protection of blacks from racial discrimination. His first Chapter opened in Atlanta during the summer of 1968 with only five people attending that first meeting. But as time went on, that single Chapter grew into two, then five, then fifty, then it spread all across the country. However, progress was measured in inches, not in miles, and the glacial pace of change began to wear him down as the years quickly ticked away.

As time went on, JJ, the civil rights activist ultimately gave way to Dr. James Johnson, the civil rights propagandist. Making noise and making money turned out to be far easier than making change. And, at some point, Dr. James Johnson had realized that a custom fit Armani suit looked and felt better than the second hand, off the rack suit that he had been wearing most of his life. Comfort had, at last, become more important than tangible results, and Dr. James Johnson had made peace with this slight change of plans.

Now, Dr. James Johnson would soon bring his sideshow antics to Orlando to do what he did best: to make some noise and to make even more money. All that Dr. James Johnson had to do now was find a way to connect with someone affected by this event. It wouldn't take long to find the perfect person.

A woman was preparing to bury both her sons. Several friends and members of her immediate family had gathered to lend their support, but Tonya Jones felt completely alone. A frail woman aged well beyond her forty-six years, Tonya did her best to raise two boys without a father; their Dad having left a few months after Curtis was born.

Working two jobs to make ends meet didn't leave a lot of quality family time for Tonya and her two boys. It was clear that, from an early age, both Calvin and Curtis would have to rely upon their own judgment when it came homework, chores, and sometimes dinner. Tonya often thought that this was no way to raise a family but, unfortunately, it was the only way that she could afford.

When Calvin started getting into trouble at school, Tonya tried desperately to change the path that he appeared to be taking in life. She often talked to Calvin about pride, perseverance, and determination, the cornerstones of a successful person. Calvin would always say, *'Yes Mama'*, but he would always return to life on the streets. Drugs, alcohol, and frustration had clouded Calvin's judgment; but a mother never gives up on her son.

Curtis was Tonya's angel. He always did well in school, and he never got into trouble in the neighborhood. Yes, Curtis had a real chance to escape the poverty of this neighborhood, but one thing stood in his way: his desire to be accepted by his brother. As Calvin's life spiraled down, Curtis was still trying to please his older brother. It was this desire to be accepted that pushed Curtis to join Calvin, and the others, that fateful night.

Oh, if only they had stayed home like I asked. Tonya thought, *I wouldn't be here planning to bury my boys.*

Outside, the press continued to wait for a statement from the family, but Tonya Jones knew that she could not say anything today, tomorrow, or anytime in the foreseeable future. The pain she felt was just too much for her to explain. As she sat there, staring at a picture of her boys, a friend paid a visit and introduced an unfamiliar face.

"This is my nephew, Daryl," the woman said.

Daryl held out his hand and said, "I'm sorry for your loss Mrs. Jones. I work for A.L.A.R.M. and Dr. Johnson. We would like to help you in any way possible."

A.L.A.R.M. was an organization that Tonya had heard of before; it was the brainchild of Dr. James Johnson, a long-time civil rights activist.

Tonya Jones asked, "What do you mean?"

"We feel that a grave injustice has been done here in Orlando," Daryl responded, "The deaths of your sons, and the other young men, are, in our opinion, a blatant attack on the good people of the Parramore district. We would like to pay for the funeral costs and offer you free legal assistance.

"Dr. Johnson, himself, will be coming here to lend you moral support and provide you, and this neighborhood, a voice that cannot be silenced by intimidation or by scorn."

Tears fell from Tonya Jones' eyes, and somewhere inside of her, the pain was slowly giving way to anger.

Now, she thought. *I might get justice for my boys.*

The next day, Tonya Jones hastily put together a press conference. As she emerged from the humble apartment that she had shared with her sons, Mrs. Jones was joined by a familiar figure. It was Dr. James Johnson, a distinguished looking black gentleman with gray hair and a gray beard.

Dr. Johnson approached the microphones and began to speak.

“We are gathered here today to support this woman, Tonya Jones. The events of last Saturday night have proven to be deeply troubling to the black people of this community. It appears as if, once again, the ugly reality of racism has cast its long shadow over the city of Orlando.

“I have heard the media label this David Taylor as the hero of the day, but I suspect that he is just a symptom of the disease that infects this city.

“I believe that the Mayor, the police department, and the majority of Orlando are attempting to push aside the undercurrent of racial discrimination that exists in this community and this nation.

“I believe that Officer Rodriguez acted in a racist manner, by following these fine young men for no good reason.

“I believe the police department is trying to protect one of its own, by discounting the story of the lone survivor, Theo Roberts.

“The deaths of Calvin Jones, Curtis Jones, William Baker, and Marcus Porter are a stain upon the state of Florida and, especially, on this city. I am here to make sure that the voices of this woman, and this community, are heard. I am here to ensure that justice is done for this woman and her two dead sons.

"Thank you, and God bless."

Although the opposition had started as a single voice, the passionate plea of an anguished mother; it had grown into a chorus of disillusioned neighbors. Ultimately, it would develop into the roar of an army, determined to seek their own version of justice. Other people from the neighborhood started to talk about racial profiling, how Officer Rodriguez had no legitimate reason to follow these fine young men, and that I had absolutely no reason to shoot them down like dogs.

♦♦♦

In the midst of the verbal assault being waged by Mrs. Jones and Dr. Johnson, a new and more dangerous threat quietly paid a visit to Orlando. Several legal representatives of a certain national gun advocacy organization had arranged a little meeting with the Mayor. Soon after their arrival at city hall, the Mayor's secretary, Betty White, escorted the secretive group to the private office of the Mayor.

Betty, an older woman with gray hair and glasses, looked more like a librarian than a trusted member of the city's political machine. This meeting would be unofficial, but the Washington interlopers failed to consider that nothing happened in city hall without Betty's knowledge.

Betty introduced the gaggle of lawyers and then returned to her desk. Once there, she hit the speaker button and listened in on the conversation. She had missed the introductions, but she found the rest of the meeting very interesting—

Betty heard the lead lawyer say, “Recent events have the organization we represent questioning whether or not Orlando is truly a family destination.”

The Mayor replied, “Yes, well that is currently under investigation, and we are waiting for the results of that investigation.”

The lawyer responded, “We appreciate the attention to detail your police department will, no doubt, provide. However, we would like to see a conviction of this David Taylor.”

The Mayor asked, “Why?”

The lawyer continued, “Let’s just say that it is in the best interests of our client that David Taylor is prosecuted to the fullest extent of the law.”

“But what if the police decide that he is not guilty of a crime?” The Mayor inquired.

The Lawyer responded, “We would hope that you would influence that possible decision.”

“Why would I do that?” the Mayor asked.

"Because" the lawyer interjected. "We could make it very difficult for you, and this city."

The Mayor pushed back from his desk, "Are you threatening me?"

The lawyer countered, "I'm saying that we could throw our financial support behind your upcoming opponent. We could ask that none of our client's members come to Orlando for vacation. Or—"

The Mayor barked, "*Or what*?"

"We can help you get reelected," the Lawyer continued, "We can encourage our client's members to take long vacations here in your beautiful city."

Angered by the thought of interference, the Mayor sternly stated, "I do not take kindly to threats, especially in my own office—"

"This is not a threat, consider this is a request. All you have to do is stress the importance of prosecution. Don't worry about public opinion; we have enough on this David Taylor to negate any sympathy that he might garner with the general public.

"Once this event has been dealt with, our client, and its members, would be very grateful to you, both financially and politically. How does Governor sound to you?"

The Mayor rubbed his chin with his right hand, thought for a few moments.

"I won't do anything illegal, but I will encourage the prosecution of this case."

"We have every confidence in you," the lawyer stated, "I look forward to seeing you in the Governor's mansion someday."

And with that, the meeting was over. After the lawyers left, the Mayor picked up the phone and called his old friend, the District Attorney. After that call, the Mayor placed a call to another old friend, The Chief of Police.

Betty, however, picked up the phone and called her own friend, Traci Kaneko.

The Chrysalis of Theo

You knew it would happen eventually; a story of this magnitude would turn decidedly political. The Florida Department of Law Enforcement, FDLE, was asked to conduct an official inquiry to determine who was responsible for the *incident*, and what steps could be taken to ensure this type of thing would never happen again.

That just wasn't enough to satisfy most politicians— they saw an opportunity to utilize the *incident* to further advance their own agendas. On one side, the gun control advocates pointed to this event as an example of things to come. On the other side, a certain national gun advocacy group (one that I cannot mention specifically due to a pending lawsuit) called it a terrible, but isolated incident. It was a little more than one hundred hours from the actual event, and the media war machine was already firing up and getting underway.

All that was needed now to turn this story into a national crisis was a little more gasoline thrown onto the smoldering fire.

Calvin and Curtis's mom was constantly on the news, claiming that I killed her sons for no good reason. She alluded to a conspiracy to cover up the racial discrimination by OPD, and Orlando, in general.

Soon, there was talk of lawsuits and veiled threats of retribution. I understood the anger of Mrs. Jones, but I always thought that Dr. Johnson was some self-serving jackass who was more interested in promoting his own image, than engaging in any actual dialog about race relations in America.

Just a few blocks away from the hospital, Detective Welles called Detectives Miller and Baker into his office. Welles closed the door and said, "Go back and tell Theo Roberts he's got his deal."

Detective Miller, who was caught in mid-sip of his coffee, produced a fine mist of mocha as he spit out, "*What*?"

A normally quiet Baker asked, "Why would the D.A. do that?"

Welles responded, "Opie, your guess is as good as mine."

Regaining his composure, Detective Miller asked, "The D.A. is willing to put this deal in writing?"

Offended by the tone of Detective Miller, Welles retorted, "That's what I just fucking said."

Miller shook his head and added, “The D.A. must have a hard on for prosecuting Taylor.”

“That’s not my department, and if you know what’s good for you, you’ll keep that shit to yourself. Do you understand?”

Detective Miller nodded and walked out the door without saying another word. Once outside of the Office, he expressed his true feelings to Baker, “This is fucking bullshit.”

“Yeah, I agree,” Baker nodded.

Detective Miller sighed, “Alright, let’s go tell Theo Roberts that Christmas came early this year.”

Baker couldn’t believe what he was about to do. It could cost him his job, but this was very important to him. Something was wrong in the D.A.’s office, and Baker needed to tell someone. Baker thought back to when he was a beat cop and a reporter gave him her business card, saying that he could call her at any time with information.

Baker spoke up, “Wait a minute, I’ve got make a call first.”

Detective Miller asked, “Can’t you do it on the way?”

“No, it’s a personal call,” Baker replied.

Already annoyed with the whole day, Detective Miller growled, "Fine, whatever. I'll be down at the car when you're ready."

Baker sat down at his desk, opened a desk drawer, pulled out an address book, and flipped thru the pages until he found the number he was looking for. Then, picking up the phone, he dialed the number and waited for an answer, but the call went to voicemail.

Baker waited for the tone and said— "Hello Traci. This is Detective Ryan Baker; I am working on the downtown shooting investigation. Something weird is going on in D.A.'s office, please give me a call whenever you get a chance."

♦♦♦

About ten minutes later, Detective Baker finally joined Detective Miller at the car. As Miller opened the driver's door, he sarcastically asked, "Did you get permission from your mother to do your fucking job?"

Detective Baker, who wasn't in the mood for such banter, silently got into the car and then closed the door. As Miller drove, Baker tried to convince himself that this deal for Roberts was the right thing to do, yet Baker clearly could not. Still conflicted about this course of action, Baker finally asked, "Why are we doing this?"

Miller replied, "Not my circus, not my monkeys."

Baker responded, "This isn't right, we shouldn't be doing this."

Miller said, "It's part of the job, making deals with bad people to get worse people off the streets."

Baker asked, "So, do you really believe that Taylor is a *worse* guy than Roberts?"

Miller stated, "No, but it's what the D.A. wants done."

Baker declared, "This is not about justice, this is about…politics."

Miller scoffed, "Of course, it's about politics…and if you don't like it, then become a politician. Otherwise, shut the fuck up and just do your job!"

Baker sat in silent contemplation for the rest of the ride to the hospital. It was just better to internalize this crisis of faith than it was to let Miller interject his cynicism into the topic.

Once parked, the Detectives met an Assistant District Attorney and the trio made their way upstairs, to Theo's room. Once inside, the A.D.A. presented Theo with a very generous offer; Theo's testimony in exchange for absolution of crimes, both related to the incident and previously committed. Detective Miller quipped, "Just sign the paperwork Theo, and you can walk out of here a free man."

The callous remark did not elicit Detective Miller's expected response from Theo. Rather, Theo looked intently at the paperwork presented to him, and politely asked for time to review the offer.

Surprised, the A.D.A. said, "This offer expires in twenty-four hours. So, if I were you, I wouldn't think about it for too long."

The trio left Theo alone with his thoughts. As the group turned left, down the hallway, Detective Miller remarked, "Not what I was expecting."

The A.D.A. said, "It actually looked like Roberts didn't want to take the deal."

Although silent, Baker had finally resolved his crisis of faith. Rather than just hint at the impiety of the D.A.'s office, he would tell Traci *everything*.

Meanwhile, just out of sight, Richard Bishop patiently waited for the Detectives to board the elevator. As the doors finally closed, Richard made his way into Theo's room.

"How did it go?"

Theo looked up at Richard's face, "They offered me the deal."

Richard replied, "You don't look happy."

Theo threw the papers across the bed, "I don't want it anymore."

Intrigued, Richard probed, "Why not?"

Theo hesitated for a moment, as if searching for the right words to say, "I don't deserve it, the terrible things I've done. He…he, doesn't deserve it either."

Richard asked, "Who?"

Theo replied, "The guy who shot me. What's his name…"

Richard stated, "David…David Taylor, I believe."

Theo nodded in agreement, "Yeah, that sounds right. He don't deserve what they want to do to him."

Richard inquired, "Why do you say that?"

Theo shook his head in dismay, "Man, CJ was gonna kill that cop. I'm sure that cop has a wife, and a family, and CJ was gonna take that all away… over a fucking robbery."

Richard delved deeper into Theo's motivation, "Didn't you try to kill David Taylor?"

Theo nodded in agreement as Richard continued, "And you're paralyzed because this David shot you, right?"

Again, Theo nodded, but said nothing. Pushing forward, Richard asked, "Knowing that you will never walk again, doesn't that bother you?"

Theo smiled, "Nah, nothing but respect for this Taylor guy."

Very pleased with the direction of this conversation, Richard asked, "Why is that?"

Theo, with purpose, looked Richard directly in the eyes, "Because he did what I shoulda done."

Richard asked, "And what was that?"

"Stopped CJ. No matter what it took, I shoulda stopped CJ…"

"Are you going to take the deal?" Changing topics, Richard questioned.

Theo shook his head, "Nah, I need to own up to what I did."

Richard smiled, "What if you took the deal, and then gave them nothing in return?"

Confused, Theo asked, "What do you mean?"

Richard started, "What do you remember about that night?"

Theo replied, "Everything. Man, I remember it all."

Richard replied, "Are you the same person that you were on that Saturday night?"

Theo stated, "Nah, I've changed."

Richard continued his train of thought, "But they are offering the deal to you, the new Theo, not the old Theo."

Perplexed, Theo responded, "What are you saying?"

Richard produced a wry smile.

"Tell them what the *new* Theo would say, tell them what you just told me. Nothing more."

Still trying to put the pieces of the puzzle together in his mind, Theo said, "I still don't know what you mean."

Richard replied, "Tell them the truth, according to the new Theo. You will honor your commitment to tell the truth, but it does nothing to help them prosecute this, David Taylor."

Theo smiled in recognition of his improbable transition from a caterpillar into a butterfly.

I Think We Should Begin Seeing Other People

The love affair was definitely over, and a cold hard reality was beginning to set in; it felt like someone was trying to destroy me. I felt as if there was a concerted effort to discredit me in the media. For some odd reason, initial reports had called me a hero for getting involved; but lately other reports were beginning to emerge that made me look more like a murderous, bloodthirsty villain.

I was credited with doing a lot of things. Some of them real: shooting five people with a wounded officer's gun found lying on the sidewalk (not what I would consider a positive thing); and some of them just not true. For example, after making an innocent CJ beg for his life, I shot him in cold blood anyway.

Details of my past, including drug use, sexual conquests, and teenage antics were beginning to bubble up to the surface.

People that I had not seen, or heard from, in years were regaling the media with wild tales of my youth, none of which made me look particularly good to the general public. It seemed that each time someone else told another story of my youth, they used creative license to embellish and exaggerate the real facts of the case in order to support their opinion of the *incident*.

Now, with allegations of racism coming to the surface, what was needed was an actual unbiased witness, someone, or more exact, something that was incapable of lying. What the world needed was a video that accurately depicted the event, from start to finish, but I couldn't wait for one to show up. I felt like I was on the defensive, and that I needed to regain some support. So, I scheduled my next, and, as it would turn out, my last public news conference. The questions were much harder this time around.

A random reporter asked, "Do you feel any remorse for killing four young black men just coming into the prime of their lives?"

Trying to stay calm, I replied, "I am sorry for the loss of life, but I felt at the time it was the only thing that I could do to save the life of Officer Rodriguez."

Another reporter theorized, “So you are saying that the life of one Hispanic Police Officer is more important that the lives of four black men?”

Already starting to get annoyed, I took another deep breath and said, “No, I am not saying that. I wish that things had turned out differently; I wish that not a single shot had been fired that night. What I am saying is that I regret there had to be any loss of life.”

Another random reporter requested, “Did the large amount of alcohol you consumed that night encourage you to make such a reckless decision?”

I was now well past annoyed and heading toward outright hostility, but again, I took a couple of more deep breaths before answering,

“I made a split-second decision, and I still stand by that decision; sober or not.”

Another random reporter shouted, “Do you feel that you should be prosecuted for the crimes that you have committed?”

OK, I had lost all patience with this line of questioning; my demeanor was starting to change.

“I don’t feel that I have committed any crimes.”

The cacophony that followed my response emphasized just how much this crowd had changed over the last few days. Another reporter called out, “How long have you been a racist?”

That was it, the very moment when I lost control of my temper, “I am not a racist!”

There, in the back of the room, unnoticed by me, stood Tonya Jones and Dr. James Johnson.

“Why did you murder my sons?”

Well, I did not expect to see them here, but there they were, and the question clearly caught me off-guard as I struggled to regain my composure.

“I do not call it murder. Your sons were about to kill Officer Rodriguez.”

A teary-eyed Tonya Jones continued, “You don’t know that for sure.”

Though confident in my actions on that night, I, somehow, missed the mark,

“One son had just shot Officer Rodriguez in the back. He then stepped up and pointed his gun at the back of Officer Rodriguez’s head; these facts cannot be disputed. There were plenty of witnesses who have testified that he did these things.

“I felt that I had no other choice. I shot your other son because he charged at me, and I was in fear of my life. I am truly sorry for your loss, but I will not call what I did murder. Next question please.”

The tension was so thick in the air that one could have cut it with a butter knife. Yet, Rhonda Spears, forever the antagonist, made the situation much, much worse, for me anyway.

“How does your daughter feel about what you have done?” she inquired.

Stunned by the accusation, I defiantly stated, “I do not have a daughter.”

Throwing a metaphorical upper-cut, Rhonda Spears smiled with delight.

“According to my sources, your daughter is now twelve years old and lives in New York. Did you deliberately abandon your daughter as an infant, or did you simply ‘forget’ about her?”

I buckled under the intensity of this exchange, “I have no idea what you are talking about. Where did you get your information?”

Rhonda reached deep inside and let loose a figurative haymaker, “From your daughter’s mother.”

Now visibly dazed and confused, I tried to fight back; but it was no use. The best that I could manage was a weak, “Who?”

Having set it up nicely, Rhonda went for the knockout punch, “Your daughter’s mother, Jane.”

Down and out for the count, I tossed in the towel. I desperately sought to end this debacle, “To the best of my knowledge I have never fathered a child. This press conference is now over. Thank You.”

And with that I stormed, well actually, wheeled, my way out of the conference room.

♦♦♦

Since the beginning of this ordeal, Terry had been serving as my unofficial press secretary and spokesman. Terry quietly kept Chris and Lynn up to date regarding my medical status. They, in turn, would pass on that information to Robyn.

My parents were there, but once it was fairly clear that I would survive, my dad, the workaholic, made plans to return to work. My mom was far too emotional and distraught to be able to rationally discuss my status with the press. So, with my parents' permission, Terry stepped up and officially took over the role.

It was a role that was well suited for him since Terry had such a quick wit and an infectious personality. Like I said before, Terry was a natural born salesman, and what I needed, right now, more than anything else, was someone willing to sell my side of the story to the press.

At some point during the press conference, someone had handed Terry a folded note. He opened the note and read what it said:

> *"Tell David that we need to talk, privately. There are things happening that he needs to know about before it's too late. Call me on my cell phone anytime, day or night.*
>
> *Thanks,*
>
> *Traci Kaneko"*

During the media melee, Terry refolded the note and placed it in his pocket. Then, as we left the press conference, Terry handed it to me and waited for me to read it.

“What do think?” Terry asked, “Is she sincere, or is she trying to get an exclusive?”

“I don’t know,” I replied, “Please call her and see want she has to say.”

“Sure, I’ll call her. Now, what’s this about a daughter?” Terry requested.

“I’m not sure. The reporter mentioned Jane.

“Listen, I’m going to tell you something that maybe two or three other people would even know about. I mean, I haven’t even told Chris about it. I did date a Jane about thirteen years ago and she moved away to New York. Before she left, we broke up, and she did tell me that she was pregnant and that she wanted money for an abortion.”

Seeking details, Terry asked, “What did you do?”

“I told her that I had the money, all she had to do was come and get it.”

Terry pleaded for more information, “Did she?”

I replied, “No, she never did. She moved away a month later.”

Rapt with anticipation, Terry continued, “What happened next?”

I resumed my confession.

"After a couple of months, I asked Rachel, one of Jane's friends, if she really was pregnant. Rachel said no. It wasn't enough for me to hear it second hand, so I asked Rachel to give me Jane's phone number so I could talk to her myself.

"I called Jane a couple of days later and asked her directly if she was pregnant. She flatly said no, she told me that she made up the story because she was mad at the time and wanted to hurt me."

Terry persisted, "Did you believe her?"

"Yeah, so I never gave it another thought… until now."

"What are you going to do about it?" Terry asked.

I said, "I don't know. As if I don't have enough going on, now I've just found out I might be a father. My head hurts, I've got to lie down for a while.

"Call me after you talk to Traci Kaneko."

Terry reassured me, "I'll let you know what she has to say. Get some sleep."

Terry lit up a cigarette as he walked out of the hospital and into the midmorning sun. He took a deep drag and held it in for a minute; it was going to be a long day. He pulled out his cell phone and dialed the number.

The phone rang a couple of times and then the voice on the other end said, “This is Traci Kaneko, can I help you?”

Terry started the conversation.

“Traci, my name is Terry. I am calling on behalf of David Taylor.”

Disappointed that it wasn’t me, Traci said, “I wanted to talk to David.”

Terry countered, “He asked me to call you for him. What is it that you want to talk about?”

Regrouping, Traci answered, “It’s important that I talk to David as soon as possible.”

“Listen, tell me what you want, and I’ll give him the information. As you can imagine, he’s not wanting to talk to a whole lot of people right now, especially members of the press.”

“There are things going on that he should know about.” Traci replied.

“Like what?” Terry asked.

Pressing the issue, Traci added, “Listen, this is something that I would like to do in person.”

“Then I’ll meet you.” Terry responded.

“With David?” Traci asked.

"No, it would be just me," Terry replied, "That's the best you're gonna get. You have to talk to me before David will talk to you. That's just the way it is. The press hasn't been extremely friendly lately to David. He's my friend, and I don't want my friend to suffer any more than he has this week. Can you understand that?"

Surprised by Terry's candor, Traci relented, "Yes, I can. How soon can we meet?"

Terry looked at his watch and said, "Anytime this afternoon is good for me."

Trying to build rapport, Traci asked, "Okay, would you like to meet for lunch?"

"Sure, where at?" Terry asked.

Traci inquired, "Do you know where Dexter's is in Winter Park?"

"Yes, I do," Terry answered.

Looking at the clock on her desk, Traci asked "How about one then?"

Terry agreed, "That's fine. I'll meet you there."

Traci could barely contain her excitement, "Until then."

Terry crushed out his cigarette; he wasn't sure what to make of the conversation he just had. Was Traci trying to work an angle, or did she really have something important to say? It had been more than a day since Terry had really had a decent meal; he was looking forward to having at least good lunch out of this meeting.

Terry climbed into his car and headed home. He had just enough time to take a shower, and then head over to Dexter's. On the way to lunch, the gravity of the situation began to spill through the valiant façade that he had erected for my benefit. However, now alone with his thoughts, Terry began to question this course of action.

Could Traci be trusted? Should she be trusted?

Somewhere in the back of Terry's mind, he vaguely remembered a politician saying, '*If you are not moving forward, you are moving backward.*' Still suspicious of Traci's motives, Terry decided that this was my best chance to move forward.

♦♦♦

It was a little after one when Terry arrived; the hostess greeted him and asked, "How many in your party?"

"I'm meeting someone for lunch," he replied.

The hostess asked, “Maybe they have already been seated. What’s your name?”

“Terry.”

The hostess looked down at the list and said, “Your party is already waiting for you. Please follow me.”

The hostess led Terry to the back of the restaurant, and there, sitting in the corner booth, was Traci Kaneko. She had a stack of papers she was shuffling through as she was sipping a glass of tea. As the hostess approached, Traci looked up and said, “Nice to finally meet you, Terry. Please sit down.”

Terry nodded and took a seat across from Traci. “Could I please have a glass of water?” he asked the hostess.

The hostess replied, “I’ll let your waitress know.”

Terry began, “What is it that you want?”

“I have some information that might be useful for David,” Traci said.

“What kind of information?” Terry requested.

Traci seemed as if she was about to answer when the waitress arrived with Terry’s glass of water. As the waitress set the water in front of Terry, she methodically spoke, “Hi, my name is Holly, and I’ll be your server today. Are you ready to order?”

Traci replied, "Yes, I'll have a house salad with the house dressing."

Holly turned to Terry and asked, "And for you, sir?"

Without even looking at the menu, Terry ordered the pan seared ahi tuna.

"Any appetizers or drinks?" Holly asked.

"Just some more tea," Traci replied.

Without a word, Holly turned and walked way. It was again just Traci and Terry staring at each other. Terry broke the silence again, "What kind of information?"

Choosing her words very carefully, Traci leaned across the table and half-whispered, "There is more going on here than you know. I have some information that would be useful to David, however—"

"How much will this information cost?" Terry interrupted.

"It's not for sale," Traci defiantly stated.

"Then what do you want?" Terry demanded.

Alarmed by Terry's bluntness, Traci responded.

"Nothing like getting to the point. Okay, I want exclusive rights to interview David."

"What is this information?" Terry asked.

Traci pushed, "Do we have a deal?"

"Before I can speak for David, I need to know what you know."

More confident than ever that she had finally set the hook, Traci cleverly proposed, "What if I were to say that I have a couple of inside sources, either of which can provide me with details that are not readily available to the general public, would you be interested?"

"From today's press conference," Terry scoffed, "It sounds like someone's already got the inside information and *is* sharing it with the general public."

"Yes," Traci hesitated for effect, "But I know who, and I know why. Sort of."

Damnit! Why the fuck would you say that?

Confused, Terry asked, "Sort of? What does that mean?"

From the corner of his eye, Terry could see Holly heading in their direction. He took a sip of water and waited for lunch to be served. Holly first placed the salad in front of Traci, and then the tuna in front of Terry.

Almost without pausing to wait for an answer, Holly stoically inquired, "Is there anything else that I can get you?"

Both Traci and Terry said no. Terry addressed their unfinished business between bites of his tuna, "If you have something worthwhile, let's hear it."

"Let me ask you something, Terry. Have you wondered why all this negative and controversial information is suddenly coming to the surface about David and his past?"

"Yes, I have." Terry answered.

After pausing to chew on her salad, Traci continued.

"The day after David's first news conference, a secret meeting took place between the Mayor and a handful of legal representatives from a certain gun rights organization…"

"So?" Once again, Terry interrupted Traci.

Finding her poise again, Traci stated— "At this meeting, they discussed how to handle the situation. It was made painfully obvious that this incident could potentially hurt Orlando, economically and politically. It was also strongly suggested to the Mayor that David be prosecuted, and it was also hinted that damaging evidence and conjecture should be used to discredit David, and to suppress any public sympathy that he might generate."

Terry asked, "Can you prove any of this?"

Full of confidence, Traci added, "Tomorrow, they are going to release portions of the city's surveillance camera system. According to one of my sources, the still pictures will show David just before he shot Calvin Jones in the head. Other still pictures will show Officer Rodriguez tailing the three suspects. Nothing else will be made available for the general public to view."

Suspicious of Traci's motives, Terry asked, "Do you have any more information?"

With conviction, Traci responded, "Yes. Do we have a deal?"

"If these so-called still pictures are released tomorrow, as you say, then yes, we have a deal," Terry nodded.

Lunch was now over, and Holly came with the check, "Was everything to your satisfaction?"

"Yes," Traci said. She took the tab and handed Holly her credit card.

"I'll be back in one moment with your receipt," Holly flashed a well-rehearsed smile.

"Traci, if what you say is true," Terry mused, "Then why do you want to help David? Why not expose the details of that meeting on tonight's news?"

Traci let down her guard for a moment as she said, "As a reporter, you're not supposed to get emotionally involved, but my uncle was a cop in New York City, and somebody shot him. I wish somebody had been there to help him; instead, he died there on a city street.

"I believe that David did the right thing, and I believe that people are trying to ruin him just for political reasons. I cannot, in good conscience, let the politically connected destroy David's life for doing the right thing. I think that I can help David *and* expose those so willing to compromise our political and legal system."

Holly came back with the receipt, "Please sign the receipt. The bottom copy is for you; thank you for coming to Dexter's and have a nice day."

Traci and Terry stood up, Traci held out her hand and Terry shook it.

"It's been a pleasure meeting you, Terry," she said.

Terry replied, "I hope to see you again."

They left together and then went their separate ways. Terry came back to the hospital to inform me of the nature of the meeting. I held my head; that headache was getting bigger by the minute, and there was no end in sight.

"Tomorrow. We will know for sure. Let's worry about it then," Terry comforted.

♦♦♦

About the same time, a few miles away, Officer Rodriguez waited to meet with The Chief of Police. Rodriguez was eventually led into the private office of the Chief. Expecting a large contingent of legal and administrative participants, Rodriguez was surprised to only see the Chief. Although the Chief was on the phone, he held his hand over the receiver upon seeing Officer Rodriguez.

"Paul, come on in and sit down please."

Officer Rodriguez took a seat in the chair and waited. After a few minutes, the Chief said, "Sorry about that. How are you feeling today?"

"A little sore still, but much better."

"Good. Good. Listen Paul, about what happened the other night," the Chief started, "It would be best if you did not discuss the incident with anyone right now. It is a touchy subject with the Mayor, and he has said that any press leaks will lead to termination."

Officer Rodriguez's eyebrow hitched, "Sir?"

The Chief replied, "If you discuss this event with anyone other than Detective Welles, you will be fired."

"Why?" Officer Rodriguez requested an explanation.

The Chief continued, "The Mayor is afraid of what any additional publicity might do to the economy. We simply cannot afford for you to say anything to anyone at this time. Do you understand my meaning?"

"Yes—" Officer Rodriguez hesitantly replied.

Interrupting, the Chief said, "Good, then this meeting is over."

The Chief stood up and shook Officer Rodriguez's hand, then the Chief sat back down, picked up the phone, and said flatly, "You can let yourself out, Paul."

Officer Rodriguez left the office as the Chief started to call back his old friend, The Mayor.

We Are Agreed

Tomorrow came, and as promised, the still pictures were released. I angrily said, "Call Traci and let her know that we have a deal."

Terry picked up his cell phone and dialed Traci's number. She answered, and Terry confirmed our commitment. He held his hand over the receiver and asked me, "When can we meet?"

"Tell her today; as soon as possible. I need to know what I'm up against."

Terry responded, "She'll be here in one hour."

I wasn't listening anymore; I was focused on the segment now on the news. There on the TV screen, giving an interview was Jane. The volume was down, so I missed the first few things that she said, but I turned up the volume just in time to hear her declare that I was indeed the father of Stacey, her twelve-year-old daughter. She explained that Stacey was born after Jane had moved to New York, and that I *did* know about the pregnancy, and subsequent birth.

Jane also said that I had shown no interest in being a part of Stacey's life and that Jane did not try to force me to be a reluctant father. Jane concluded her interview by saying that she felt no malice toward me; however, she was disappointed in my decision when it came to my lack of involvement in Stacey's life. Stunned, I just sat there with my mouth open, not knowing what to do, or to think. Terry took the remote out of my hands and turned off the TV.

"I think you've seen enough news for today," Terry said,

Minutes went by as if in slow motion; dazed by what I had just seen, I still could not speak. Terry looked me in the eyes and said, "Pull it together, David, Traci will be here soon. You can worry about this Stacey thing later; we've got to figure what to do right now."

Moments later, Traci entered the room. I was surprised that she was alone, without a cameraman or a video recorder. As I sat there, mostly catatonic, Terry explained the Jane interview, and apologized for my less than friendly demeanor. Traci looked at me, snapped her fingers in my face, and said, "Snap out of it. We need to talk."

This caught my attention, "About what?"

Traci replied, “We need to develop a strategy to handle this situation.”

I nodded in agreement and asked, “What can we do?”

“First,” Traci said. “No more press conferences. We need to rebuild your public image. An exclusive interview, in a controlled environment, discussing your perspective at the time of the incident; then mix in some positive comments on video from friends and family, and finally, we need to exploit the criminal records of the young men in question.”

That sounded like a really good plan of action, so I nodded in agreement.

“Do you have a lawyer?” Traci asked.

“No, I do not,” I answered.

“You need one, now. I know the perfect person for you, she is a friend of mine, and she is a very good lawyer. I’ll give you her name and number so you can set up an appointment with her.”

“I can’t afford a good lawyer.” I stated.

“Just talk with her and see what she can do,” Traci responded, “I believe that this is the type of case she would have a very hard time passing on, regardless of the cost.”

“Anything else?” I asked.

“Have you talked with the police lately?” Traci inquired.

Hesitating, I said, “Maybe three or four times since the beginning of this, why?”

Traci said directly, “Stop talking to the police without a lawyer present. Everything you have said will be used against you when they try to prosecute you. Remember, they are trying to paint you as the bad guy in this whole situation. When a trail begins, they will take advantage of all the information that you have given them. What have you told the police?”

I replied, “The truth, more or less. I have told them about my involvement, but I have been very reluctant to reveal who else was with me that night, other than Terry.”

Intrigued, Traci asked, “Why?”

I said, “There were people who were there who I do not want to involve in this.”

Again, Traci asked, “Why?”

I responded— “A couple of them are married and have a family; I do not want to disrupt their lives any more than I have with this. So far, the press and police have interviewed them, and they do admit to being downtown, but they deny being present at the time of the shooting. I would like it to stay that way.”

"I can understand that," Traci nodded, "We need to discuss this Stacey issue. Did you know about her before this week?"

"No, I did not. Jane even told me years ago that she made up the story to hurt me."

"Then why is Jane saying something different today?"

Confused, I said, "I don't know. I need to talk to her."

"Don't, at least not until you have a lawyer, then let the lawyer contact Jane. Are there any other surprises out there that I should know about? For example, who is this mystery woman the police are looking for?"

"I can't tell you," I answered.

"Why not?" Traci asked.

"I will not allow her to be dragged into this."

"Listen," Traci sighed, "*You are going to have to trust me. Otherwise, this will not work.*"

"I'm having a hard time trusting just about anybody in the press," I admitted, "Terry's belief that you can help me is the only reason that you are here right now. At least, for the time being, can't we just get around her involvement? Let's just say that she wasn't supposed to be there, and it will ruin her life if the truth comes out."

“Well, the police are not going to stop looking for her,” Traci retorted.

It was at that time Terry spoke up, “What if…”

I looked at Terry and asked, “What if what?”

“What if we said it was Jill? The police are looking for a girl, right? Then let’s say that it was Jill who was pleading for you not to die.”

“But why would your sister do that?” I asked.

“Because she knows how good of friends we are,” Terry replied, “She could say that she got caught up in the moment and was worried about how it would affect my life if you died.”

“Traci, do you think that they would buy that?” I asked.

“No, I wouldn’t recommend that at all. I would advise that you tell the truth…”

I asked Terry, “Would Jill agree to this?”

Terry said, “I’m sure that she will.”

“Can she be believable? Will she sound sincere?” I pushed.

“Yes, I believe that she can.”

I looked at Traci, “When should do we do this interview?”

Traci said, “I want you to first get a lawyer. After that, I’ll leave it up to you, however, the sooner the better.”

Traci wrote down the name and number of the attorney that she suggested. Before leaving, she said, “I would call her today if I were you. You can call me anytime day or night; I’ll make myself available to you, or Terry, whenever you are ready.

“If there is anything you need, then please give me a call. Thank you for seeing me.”

Traci shook my hand and then Terry’s, and with a quick turn she left out the door.

I looked at the piece of paper that Traci had just handed me. In an elegant and distinct cursive writing was the name *Alice Miller, Attorney*. I picked up the phone and called the number. After a couple of rings someone answered—

“Alice Miller’s office, this is Debbie, can I help you?”

“Hi Debbie, my name is David Taylor. Traci Kaneko said that I should give Alice a call, is she available?”

“Please hold for one minute.”

Twenty seconds elapses—

“This is Alice Miller. Mister Taylor how may I help you?”

"Alice, can I call you Alice?"

Alice replied, "Please do."

I continued, "Alice, Traci Kaneko gave me your name and number. She suggested that I seek the counsel of an attorney and she assured me that you were the perfect person for the job. Would you be interested in discussing my case?"

"Absolutely," Alice confidently replied.

"When could we meet?" I asked with trepidation.

"I can meet you anytime and anyplace you wish." Alice said.

"I would like to do this as soon as possible. Could you come by the hospital this afternoon?"

"Sure. What time would be good for you?"

I looked at the clock on the wall; it was now a little after ten in the morning. I said, "How about two this afternoon?"

"I'll be there," Alice said, "And Mister Taylor? Thank you for allowing me the opportunity to meet with you."

"Don't thank me, yet," I said.

Ignoring my attempt at humor, Alice said, "I'll see you at two. Goodbye Mister Taylor."

I replied, "Please call me David."

Alice said, "Goodbye, David. I'll see you at two."

♦♦♦

I wasn't sure what to expect; I've never needed to talk to a lawyer before, and I've never known one personally. For the next few hours, it was all I could think about, how would this meeting go? Would she accept my case despite my obvious lack of funds? Was she really a good attorney?

It was now almost two in the afternoon, and I wouldn't have to wait much longer. It was about five minutes to two when I got a call announcing the arrival of Alice Miller. When she entered the room, something inside me told me that she was the right lawyer for me. Tall and thin, with long black hair, Alice exuded professionalism. She walked over, stuck out her hand, and introduced herself.

"David, I'm Alice Miller. It's a pleasure to meet you in person." She then turned to Terry, "Terry, I presume. Traci has told me how good of a friend you are to David. I hope I can live up to the high standard of trust and dedication that you, and others, have exhibited during this ordeal."

It was then that I first learned the value of an outstanding lawyer and their uncanny knack for knowing not just what to say, but how to say it. I started the conversation—

“Alice, I’m glad that you would meet with me on such short notice.”

Alice replied, “David, again it’s my pleasure to meet with you. “

“Alice, I don’t know quite how to say this, but I don’t know if I can afford your services. How much per hour do you charge?”

“Normally I do charge by the hour, but in a case like yours, David, I charge a standard flat fee. I find that a flat fee is easier, and more productive, than trying to account for every minute spent researching and developing a solid defense strategy.”

“That’s great, but how much?” I asked.

“Typically, for a case of this magnitude, I would charge a minimum of two-hundred and fifty-thousand, in advance, not including the fees for expert testimony or other expenses.”

Stunned by the amount, I gasped, “There’s no way I could raise that kind of money right now.”

“I completely understand,” Alice responded, “So, let me make a proposal to you David. I will only charge you twenty-five-hundred dollars, that you can pay in installments of any amount, whenever convenient and possible for you.”

"That's more than fair, but why would you do that for me?" I asked.

"Because I believe in what you did. It was a difficult decision to make in such a short amount of time, and you acted without regard for your own safety to help a threatened law enforcement officer. I respect that."

Rebounding from the sticker shock, I declared, "Thank you for your generosity, but I have another question. I don't know how to phrase it without it sounding, well…stupid. But as a black woman, do you have a problem representing a person who has recently been labeled in the press as a 'racist'?"

"Are you a racist?" Bluntly, Alice proposed.

"No," I said.

"Would you have done the same thing if they were white?" Alice asked, delving deeper into my motivation.

"Yes," I replied.

"Then why would I have a problem representing you? This incident was not about race, it was about saving the life of a fellow human being. White or black, it would not have changed the outcome, nor would it have altered your actions. So, I see no reason why the race of the obviously guilty criminals should have any bearing on this event."

Amazed with Alice's gift for speaking, I asked, "When can you start?"

"I already have."

She smiled at me, "Now, if you don't mind, I'd like to hear everything that has happened, from your point of view. Please keep in mind that whatever you tell me will be kept in the strictest of confidence between attorney and client. I will not divulge any information discussed to anyone without your prior knowledge and approval."

Terry and I began to tell the story of the evening in question. We didn't hold back any details, including the presence of Robyn and our decision to keep her involvement secret. We discussed our idea of using Jill as the mystery girl the police were looking for. However, Alice discouraged that approach saying the chances of Robyn's identity being revealed by someone else were extremely high. She said that, by covering up the truth, it would make us look deceitful and untrustworthy in the eyes of a jury.

Alice requested permission to approach Robyn and see if she would voluntarily reveal her presence at the scene. I told Alice that it was fine for her to ask Robyn to come forward, but if Robyn decided not to admit to being present then we would proceed with the Jill cover story.

After spending a great deal of time on the actual event, we went on to discuss the current news coverage and the reasons behind my negative portrayal in the press. Based on the information provided by Traci, it seemed to Alice that there was a concerted effort to destroy my reputation, and in effect, limit the amount of support that I might receive from the general public.

Alice was convinced that the biased media coverage was born out of political considerations and that it would only increase without a careful and calculated media counterattack. She suggested that, since I was not comfortable in live situations, I should resort to taped interviews and written responses to blunt the effectiveness of my opposition's media campaign.

A more immediate concern to Alice was the accusations by Jane regarding my knowledge of Stacey, and my lack of involvement in Stacey's life. Any indictment would be weeks away, and an actual trial would be at least six months, maybe a year later. Alice recommended that I seek a paternity test before responding Jane's allegations. I expressed my interest in talking directly with Jane, but Alice discouraged that course of action until it was proven that I was, indeed, the biological father of Stacey.

We agreed that Alice would first contact Jane and then request a paternity test. It was a calculated risk, considering the possibility of being perceived as a cold and callous father, but it was an issue that needed to be resolved one way or another, and very quickly.

Hours had gone by in what felt like mere minutes. It was well past 6 PM when we finally finished our first consultation. As Alice was saying her goodbyes, I found myself finally able to relax, just a little. I had been on edge since the *incident*; and the recent news coverage coupled with the revelation of Stacey had pushed me well beyond an uncontrolled panic. However, for the first time in a week, I actually felt the panic level drop down to an almost manageable level.

After Alice was gone, Terry and I discussed what information to pass on to Chris, Lynn, Jill, and Robyn. We agreed on the basic steps to take next, but we disagreed about Robyn's involvement and how it should be handled. I felt that it was important to stress to Robyn that it was her decision to come forward publicly. Terry felt that Alice was right, and that it was important for Robyn to step up now before someone else could identify her. I reminded Terry that he was just to pass on the information that Robyn would be contacted by Alice, and not to try to convince Robyn to come forward herself.

Terry left for the night, only stopping just outside the hospital front doors to light up a cigarette, before pulling out his cell phone and beginning the process of contacting everyone. He didn't stop to notice that there was a beautiful full moon slowly coming up over the horizon. The long day had ended, but there was still so much more work to do. Terry was very tired now, but he had a friend—me—to look out for, and that was more important to him than a couple hours of sleep.

Hello Robyn, it's me, Alice

The next morning, Alice was determined to speak with Robyn. She knew that it was a calculated risk, but Alice picked up the office telephone and then dialed Robyn's number anyway. After a few rings, a disheveled voice answered, "Hello?"

"Hi, is this Robyn?" Alice asked.

"Yes, it is. Who is this?" Robyn replied.

"My name is Alice Miller; I am David Taylor's attorney. Can we talk?" Only silence replied. Alice spoke again. "Are you still there?"

"Yes." Robyn responded, "I'm just surprised to hear from you this soon."

"Time is of the essence. Any type of delay could be detrimental to David's defense. Can we talk?"

"Yes, but not over the phone," Robyn nervously agreed, "I would like to meet you in person first."

"That would be fine with me," Alice cautiously replied, "Most people never want to meet with an attorney, can I ask you why meeting me is important to you?"

Ignoring the question, Robyn pushed, "We can talk about that later. When and where would you like to meet?"

Alice continued, "The sooner the better. How about this afternoon in my office?"

"Where is your office located?" Robyn asked.

Alice responded, "The address is one-zero-five East Robinson Street, I'm on the second floor. Do you know where Robinson Street is?"

Robyn replied, "I'll find it. I can be there in two hours; would that work for you?"

"Absolutely, I will see you then," Alice concluded.

Robyn hung up the phone without even saying goodbye.

Alice had some time to kill, so she began working on a letter to send to Jane. It covered the usual information*: my client this; my client that, cease and desist, please submit to a DNA test*…the list went on and on. She had just about finished the letter when she got word that Robyn had arrived. She instructed her receptionist to show Robyn in. As Robyn entered the room, Alice stood up, held out her hand.

"You must be Robyn. Please come in and sit down."

Robyn shook her hand and took a seat in the chair across from Alice's desk.

Alice began, "How are you today?"

"I'm a nervous wreck, Mrs. Miller," Robyn replied.

"Please call me Alice," Alice responded, "Why are you such a nervous wreck?"

Robyn countered, "Because, *Alice*, my best friend is lying in a hospital bed, and there is absolutely nothing I can do about it."

Alice alluded, "Maybe we can remedy that situation. I would like to discuss with you today your activities on the night in question."

"First, I would like to ask you a few questions, *Alice*," Robyn's tone was less than friendly.

"Please do. I'll answer any question that I can."

Genuinely curious, Robyn continued, "How did you become involved in David's case?"

"Through a mutual friend." Alice stated.

Now very confused by Alice's response, Robyn asked, "Who?"

Dodging the question, Alice said, “I’m sorry, but I am not at liberty to say.”

“Why not?” Robyn asked.

“Client-Attorney confidentiality.”

Getting to the point, Robyn asked, “What’s in this for you? I can look around your office and I know that David could not afford your services. So why are you involved? For the publicity?”

“Why do I get the feeling that I am the one being interviewed here?” Alice smiled.

“Because you are. I don’t want David’s fate to rest in the hands of a slick attorney who doesn’t give a shit about him. How is David paying you, and why do you care about David’s plight?”

“Under normal circumstances,” Alice explained, “David could not afford my services, but we reached a financial agreement. I care about David’s legal situation because I care about David, just as you do.”

“You couldn’t possibly care about David as much as I do,” Robyn retorted.

“No, I suppose not, but what I mean to say is that I respect the decision that David made. It was a difficult decision that he made in an extremely short amount of time. It was a decision that almost cost him his life. The defense of a defenseless human being; how could I not care about David's fate? And in regard to the publicity of this case, yes that was a factor in my accepting his case, but not the only one."

Surprised by Alice's response, Robyn probed, "What else contributed to your decision to take David's case?"

"The challenge," Alice flatly answered.

"The challenge of what?" Robyn asked.

"I'm not sure how much Terry has told you, but it appears that there has been some political collusion to discredit and ultimately prosecute David. The forces that appear to be behind this personal attack on David are some of the most powerful people in the county, state, and quite possibly, even the federal government. David will need the best legal defense that he can muster, and I believe that I am capable of delivering that legal defense."

Robyn continued, "And what if you're wrong?"

"Then I will find someone better to continue the fight."

Sarcastically, Robyn scoffed, "For a great deal of more money, I'm sure."

"I feel so strongly about this case that I would pay for David's legal defense, if I felt that I could not win." Alice responded.

Robyn asked, "Why?"

"Because, like I said before, I respect the decision that David made. David is special and he did what most of us would never dream of doing; he got involved. I can see now why David means so much to you, Terry, Chris, Lynn, and many others."

"The others maybe," Robyn's demeanor noticeably changed, "But no one can understand how much, or why, he means so much to me."

Always to the point, Alice interjected, "You do still love him, don't you?"

"More than you could possibly know," Robyn had finally let her guard down and smiled.

"Will you openly admit that you were with David that night? I understand the difficulty this will cause in your personal life, but David needs you now, more than ever."

"Only if I am allowed to see him," As Robyn answered, the smile faded away.

"I think I can arrange that," Alice replied.

"Once you have, then I will come forward and admit that I am the mystery woman that everyone is looking for. I will admit my entire role in this tragic event."

Out of curiosity, Alice asked, "What will your husband say?"

"I don't know." Robyn confided.

"Does he know about you and David?"

"He suspects." Robyn replied.

Trying to assess the personal fallout from the public announcement of Robyn's involvement, Alice nudged her further, "Do you think that he might want a divorce?"

"I don't know," Robyn shrugged.

Showing her human side, Alice soothed, "Do you need time to think this over?"

"No. I would much rather see David and worry about everything else later." Robyn said.

"Would tomorrow work for you?" asked Alice.

"The sooner the better..."

Alice could clearly see the discomfort in Robyn's eyes. It wasn't fear Alice saw, it was the realization that life, as Robyn knew it, would soon be over. To change the subject, Alice asked, “By the way, did I pass your interview?”

“Let’s just say that I’m liking you so far,” Robyn replied, “You still have a long way to go before you can convince me that you believe in David as much as I do.”

“How can I do that?”

Robyn retorted, “Get him out of this mess that he is in. Call me when you have set up a time that I can visit David. Thank you for your time.”

Robyn got up and headed for the door. She didn’t even stop to say goodbye to Alice, she was much too upset to worry about formalities.

After Robyn left the office, Alice finished up her letter to Jane. She double checked the wording, signed the letter, and had her receptionist send it overnight shipping so Jane would have the letter first thing in the morning. Next, Alice got on the phone to coordinate Robyn’s arrival at the hospital. She knew that Robyn could not get past the media without a little help from a friend. Alice arranged for Robyn to come in through the employee entrance with the help of a doctor, who just happened to be on staff at the hospital.

The arrangements were made for Robyn to meet a friend in the hospital at 10 AM. Alice called Robyn and committed to the morning rendezvous, explaining all the details of where she was to go, and who would be her guide to the room.

Everything was going according to plan, so far.

A Very Busy Day

The next morning, at 9:45 AM, there was a knock at Jane's door. She hesitated for a second but regained her composure and then answered the door. The delivery driver had a letter for her.

"Please sign here," he requested. As she signed the pad, the driver said, "Thank you, Ma'am."

Then he handed her the letter, quickly turned, and walked back to his truck. Before she could even finish opening the letter, he was in the truck and driving away.

She knew what it was before she even read the letter; she knew that it was from me. Jane had been expecting a letter ever since her confession to the media; she knew that I would be contacting her soon. What she wasn't expecting was a letter from an attorney threatening legal action if she did not immediately stop saying that the child in question was mine, until such a time as a DNA test could conclusively prove that Stacey was my daughter.

The letter also demanded that Jane no longer interact with any member of the press until resolution of the matter and threatened to seek financial damages against Jane if she did not comply.

Jane was additionally instructed to provide a blood sample and a DNA sample of Stacey. This was to be supervised by an impartial medical technician or doctor within one week, so validity of her claim that I am Stacey's biological father could be verified or proven false. The letter went on to state that a negative result would lead to a lawsuit and possible criminal charges.

Jane sat down in a chair and started to cry. She knew, or more exactly, she feared, that this day would eventually come, and now it was here. She had no words to describe the terror and heartache that consumed her world.

Why the fuck did I pick up the phone? She thought to herself. *Why the fuck did I agree to do that interview?*

She wiped away the tears with her sleeve, let out a heavy sigh, and then set out in her mind to solve the problem now at hand: *How do I tell Stacey?*

About the same time that Jane got the letter, a familiar face arrived at the employee entrance to the hospital; she wouldn't have to wait long to be let inside.

Doctor Robertson opened the door and asked, "Robyn?"

Robyn nodded, and he waved her into the open door. Once inside, Robyn was quickly, and discretely, led to my room. As the door opened and she looked inside, she saw me for the first time since that Saturday night.

All that I could manage to say was, "Hi Robyn."

With tears rolling down her face, she ran over and gave me a big embrace.

"Not so hard, I still hurt a lot," I said, as I began to cry as well.

"I'm sorry," she was wiping the tears away from her eyes. "I thought I lost you."

I chuckled, "I thought you lost me too."

"I missed you so much," she hugged me again; it seemed as if time stood still—

"I missed you too," I smiled, relishing the moment and I whispered in her ear, "I love you."

She whispered back, "I love you too."

We didn't let go for at least five minutes; we were so overcome with emotion that neither of us could talk. When she finally let go, she looked at me and said, "You look like hell."

I laughed, "Thanks, I needed that."

We both laughed and then hugged again. I looked at her and said, "Alice told me what you want to do. You don't have to; I can get through this without involving you."

Stubbornly, Robyn said, "I wouldn't let you try to go through this alone."

I asked, "But what about Tom?"

"I'll worry about that later," she insisted, "Right now, you need me; and I need you. We'll worry about everything else when this is over."

In a very serious tone, I stated, "This might take a very long time."

"So what? You are worth it," she said through a broad smile.

Concerned about Robyn's future, I asked, "Thanks, but what about your marriage?"

Still smiling— "If Tom cannot deal with this, then maybe we shouldn't be together."

Still sounding serious, I said, “That’s not fair. I don’t want you to risk your marriage for me. I’m not worth that.”

“Yes, yes you are,” she stated with an unwavering conviction.

In a moment of levity, I quipped, “Liar.”

Robyn laughed and gave me a hug again. Doctor Robertson was pointing at his watch. She said, “I’ve got to go, but I’ll be back. Soon. Once my involvement is out in the open, I can visit you whenever I want.”

Serious again, I said, “I hope so.”

As we hugged one last time, I whispered into Robyn’s ear, “It’s not too late for us, we can disappear tomorrow. We can go away and pretend that this never happened.”

She looked me in the eyes and said, “Don’t tempt me, one of these days I might just take you up on that offer.”

Robyn walked out of the room, but not before she turned and blew me a kiss. Before I could respond, she was gone. It was the best I had felt in years; I could die a happy man. Unfortunately, it wasn’t meant to last.

♦♦♦

Right about the time of Robyn's hospital visit, the news released another video documenting the shooting. Rhonda Spears had received a video from a couple in England who were in Orlando on the night of the *incident*. They made a tape but didn't bother to watch it until after they returned home. Once they heard of the media coverage regarding the shooting, they decided to turn it over to a network. It just so happened that they chose a certain network, and conveniently, Rhonda Spears.

The video clearly showed me shooting CJ in the head and then shooting Calvin in the chest. The video continued to show the rest of the shootout, including the fatal shots to Willie B and Tiny. The video also showed me getting shot multiple times and ended minutes after the EMTs arrived. In the video, you could clearly see Robyn being led away by Chris and Lynn. Although there was no audio to accompany the video, it was clear to see who the mystery woman was saying, "*Please don't die. Please don't die.*"

It wasn't long after Robyn left that I had another visitor, Detective Chris Welles. We had talked three times before about the incident and I had been vague, and a little aloof, in our conversations, but he seemed like a nice guy. Today was different; he walked into the room and snapped, “So, you *did* know the mystery woman we’ve been looking for.”

My response, as supplied by Alice Miller, “I’m sorry, but I cannot speak to you without the presence of my attorney.”

Trying to control his anger, Detective Welles growled, “Look you little shit, I don’t give a fuck about you, or your attorney. *I want you to tell me the truth!*”

I smirked, “I’m sorry, but I cannot speak to you without the presence of my attorney.”

Enraged, Detective Welles shouted, “Tell me the fucking truth right now, or God help me, I’ll make your life miserable!”

I laughed, “It already is, but I’m sorry that I cannot speak to you without the presence of my attorney.”

Changing tactics, Detective Welles panted, “Fine, have it your way. I already have enough to charge you with several serious crimes. I will seek an indictment and you will be charged; that is, unless you talk to me now. Just tell me what really happened, and I’ll see what I can do about reducing and even dropping some charges.”

Again, I said, “I’m sorry, but I cannot speak to you without the presence of my attorney.”

Trying to reason with me one last time, Detective Welles pleaded, "This is your last chance, talk to me now, or I will do everything in my power to make sure that you go to jail for the better part of your life."

I said, "I'm sorry, but I cannot speak to you without the presence of my attorney."

No longer trying to hide his contempt, Detective Welles glowed red with anger.

"*Fuck you, you little shit!* I'll see that you go to jail, and we'll see how smug you are then! You're gonna end up being some nigger's little bitch when I'm through with you. Your attorney will not be able to help you avoid jail time. You will go to jail, and you will regret not cooperating with me!"

And with that, Chris Welles stormed out of the room. I just couldn't resist adding one more thing as he left; "Have a nice day."

He flicked me off and then was gone.

Meanwhile, in another part of town...

♦♦♦

It had only taken minutes after the airing of the tape, before calls began to come in identifying the mystery woman as Robyn. One of those calls came from Tom, her husband.

When Robyn got home, Tom was waiting for her. This was a surprise to Robyn because Tom should have been at work. As she walked in the door, Tom paused the video he was watching, and asked Robyn, “Is there something that you would like to tell me?”

“No, why?” Robyn replied as she walked into the Family Room. There, frozen on the TV was a frame from the video released earlier in the day by Rhonda Spears. The picture clearly showed a distressed Robyn being led away from the shooting by familiar faces. Tom again repeated, “Is there something that you would like to tell me?”

Robyn hesitated for a moment; however, Tom would not relent, *“Is there something that you would like to tell me?!”*

Robyn realized that nothing but the whole truth would suffice; she began choosing her words very carefully, “Tom, we need to talk.”

“Is that really you and are you really with *him*?” The tone was now very hostile.

Robyn tried to remain calm, “Yes, but let me explain—”

“Explain what?” Enraged, Tom shouted, “That you’ve been lying to me all these years; that you’ve been spending time with *him* and then *lying* to me about it!”

“Yes, but—” Robyn stammered.

“Have you been fucking him too?” Tom barked, blinded with jealousy.

Robyn protested, “No, now will you let me talk?”

On the verge of a meltdown, Tom screamed, “Why should I? All you’re going to do is try to make this better, and I don’t see how you can!”

Trying to defuse the situation, Robyn pleaded, “Tom, listen to me.”

“Fuck you, bitch!” Tom raised his hand back like he was going to hit her. Robyn braced for the impact that she felt was sure to come, however, he stopped himself.

“How could you do this to me? You promised me that you wouldn’t talk with David again. I trusted you; and this is how I find out, on national TV. You know my family already knows about this. People from work, my friends, everyone knows” –tears began to roll down Tom’s face— “and God damn it, I still love you.”

Robyn assured Tom, "I love you too—"

Enraged again, Tom demanded, "Then why would you do this to me?"

Looking for the right words, Robyn squeaked, "It's complicated…"

"*How?!*" Dumfounded, Tom shouted. "You said that you wouldn't talk to him again! How is that complicated?"

Ashamed, Robyn pleaded, "Tom, I really thought I could let David become part of my past."

"What happened? Wasn't I good enough for you?"

"It has nothing to do with you, Tom," Robyn replied.

His voice quivering, Tom continued seeking answers, "Then what was it?"

Robyn thought for a moment, looking for the right words to say, "David and I have a connection that is difficult to put into words."

Regaining some composure, Tom said, "Try."

"David and I…" she hesitated, still looking for the right words, "…share a connection that defies explanation."

"What the fuck does that mean?" Tom huffed.

"Tom, I love you, but David and I have always shared something that most people cannot comprehend. It is as if we are kindred spirits, with both of us providing a vital piece to complete a spiritual puzzle, one that cannot be explained using words. It is something that must be experienced to be understood," the words even sounded silly to Robyn.

Looking for some kind of logic, Tom asked, "If you two are so close, then why did you marry me?"

"Tom, our relationship is different," Robyn replied.

Incredulous, Tom asked, "How?"

Robyn said, "I love you."

Not really wanting to know the answer, Tom asked, "What about David?"

"I need him," Robyn replied.

"*What?!*"

Robyn reasoned, "He makes me a whole person, it is as if he provides a part of me that I would be lacking otherwise. He gives me strength, wisdom, and insight that I would not be able to accomplish on my own."

"What about me, can't I do those things for you?"

"Yes, but on a different level," Robyn tried again to reason with Tom.

Not sure what to think, Tom asked, "What? You don't make any sense."

Being completely honest with Tom, Robyn proposed, "Look at it this way, David has had such a profound effect on me, that if I had not met him when I did, then I would not be the person that you love today. He is a part of my life that I cannot live without."

"Where does that leave us?" Tom asked.

"Right where we've always been," Robyn responded.

"I thought we were happily married. I thought we would be together forever."

"And now?" Robyn cringed.

Without emotion, Tom said, "I'm not so sure."

"Tom, nothing has changed with us—" Robyn pleaded, but was cut short.

"Everything has changed. Until today, I thought that I was the most important person in your life. Now, I'm not sure that I even matter to you as much as David does."

Robyn pleaded, "Tom, you do."

“It doesn’t look that way to me,” Tom said coldly, “It looks to me like you married the wrong person. You should have married David if you felt so deeply about him.”

With her voice shaking, “Tom, I married you…because I love you.”

“Do you still love him?”

Robyn did not answer; she just looked down at the floor.

“That’s what I thought,” Tom said flatly, “I think it would be a good idea that you leave now.”

“When do you want me to come back?” Robyn asked.

Bluntly, Tom said, “At this point, I’m not sure that I want you back at all.”

Trying to appeal to Tom’s sensibility, Robyn pleaded, “Tom, please don’t do this.”

“Do what? It’s *you* who has caused this. Get out, before I throw you out.”

“Tom, please…” Robyn begged.

Ignoring Robyn’s plea, Tom shouted, “*No!* I don’t want to hear it! *Just go away now!*”

Robyn sobbed, “Where?”

"I don't care. If you think so much of David, then why don't you go stay with him?"

"Tom, please don't—" Robyn implored.

"Go! Before I do something that we will both regret!" Tom was now in an almost uncontrollable rage again.

Robyn gathered up a few personal belongings while Tom just sat on the couch, watching the video over and over. When Robyn was done, she tried one last time to make amends.

"Tom, I love you." Silence: she continued, "I'll call you later."

Tom bellowed, *"Don't!"*

"Tom, is our marriage over?" Robyn asked with tears running down her cheeks.

Tom laughed, "Yeah, I think so."

Sobbing uncontrollably, Robyn said, "Please don't say that."

"I'll call you if I change my mind." Tom turned his attention back to the video.

Robyn cried, "Tom, please..."

But there was no answer. Dejected, she took her things, turned, and then walked out the door. Once she got into the car, she just sat there in the driveway, crying. She didn't know what to do now.

More than one thousand miles away, another part of this saga would soon begin…

♦♦♦

Jane had since regained her composure; she called Alice Miller to discuss the letter. The phone rang a couple of times and then a woman answered.

"Thank you for calling Alice Miller's office, this is Debbie can I help you?"

Politely, Jane said, "Hi, I'd like to speak to Alice Miller please."

"Can I tell her who is calling?"

"Tell her it's Jane. Jane Sinclair."

"Please hold for a moment," the voice stated, followed by smooth jazz hold music.

Jane was on hold for a minute or so before Alice picked up the phone.

"Hello, Miss Sinclair, this is Alice Miller, the Attorney representing David Taylor in this matter. How can I be of assistance to you?"

Fidgeting in her seat, Jane answered, "Please call me Jane. Can't we avoid doing this?"

Professional and direct, Alice explained, "I'm sorry Jane, but you were the one who publicly made the accusation that David is the biological father of your daughter. This is not something that can be ignored or avoided by David."

Jane responded, "I didn't have a choice."

"What does that mean?" Alice asked.

"That reporter, Rhonda Spears, told me that if I did not voluntarily come forward and provide an interview that she would air the story anyway."

Ignoring Jane's discomfort, Alice persisted, "According to David, you lied in your interview about his knowledge of Stacey. Did you lie, or is your memory of the event less than perfect?"

After a brief moment of silence, Jane finally acknowledged the uncomfortable truth of the matter.

"Yes, I lied. Rhonda told me to. I told her off camera that I lied to David about being pregnant; she said that it would be in

Stacey's best interest if I were to present David as an uninterested father. It would be easier to explain to Stacey that David did not want to be part of her life than to explain that I did not want him to be part of her life."

Surprised by Jane's candor, Alice asked, "What did you tell Stacey about her alleged father?"

Embarrassed, Jane said, "I told her that he had died."

"So, you lied to her as well?" the disdainful tone in Alice's voice was very evident.

Offering an explanation, Jane returned, "Yes, and no. To me, my love for David had died. When Stacey was old enough to begin asking why she didn't have a father, I exaggerated the truth, a little, by saying that he was dead. I didn't bother to explain how or why he was dead."

"You do realize that if David is proven to be Stacey's biological father, he will pursue visitation rights and shared custody."

Stoically, Jane answered, "Yes."

Trying to avoid a drawn-out legal battle, Alice inquired, "Is this something that will be contested, or are you willing to quickly resolve this issue?"

Jane conceded, "Yes, I am, but I would like to speak with David directly. I would like to try and explain what I did, and why I did it."

"I'm sorry, but that will not be possible until it is proven that David is indeed the biological father of your daughter." Alice said.

Trying to illicit sympathy, Jane pleaded, "It is important that I explain my reasoning to David. I must be allowed to explain why I lied to him about Stacey."

Unimpressed with Jane's subdued demeanor, Alice countered the offer.

"Once it has been established that David is the biological father of your daughter, it would then be appropriate to discuss the specifics of your decision to exclude David from the parental rights that he would have been otherwise entitled to. It would also then be appropriate to discuss visitation and custody rights that would be available and agreeable to both parties.

"Jane, provide the requested blood and DNA samples and then we can settle this matter quickly. However, until such time that it is proven that my client is indeed the biological father of Stacey, I will not allow a direct dialog between you and David. After all, David might not be the biological father of Stacey."

In a moment of defiance, Jane responded, "David *is* Stacey's father; I don't need any test to know for sure. I will provide the requested samples, and then maybe we can resolve this issue privately."

Recognizing the change in Jane's attitude, Alice decided that it was time to end the call. "I hope that we can reach an agreement."

Sarcastically, Jane said, "Thank you for your time, Miss Miller."

With equal sarcasm, Alice replied, "Thank you for responding so quickly to my requests, Jane."

Jane wouldn't have long to plot her strategy; Stacey would be home from school in just a few hours. A terrible thought entered Jane's mind—*How do I tell my twelve-year-old daughter that I lied to her about her father? The same father that I said, so many years ago, was dead. How do I tell Stacey that her father never even knew that she existed?*

An even worse thought manifested—*How will Stacey take this confession?*

Looking for the right words to say, Jane sat at the kitchen table writing notes, scratching the words out, and then writing some more. Lost in thought, she hadn't noticed the passage of time until she heard the lock and looked up in time to see Stacey walk in the door.

"Hi, Mom!" Stacey playfully announced her return from school.

"Hi…" Jane couldn't finish her sentence, the weight of what was to come next had crushed her voice. Tears, once again, began streaming down her cheeks.

A visibly worried Stacey asked, "Mom, what's wrong?"

Jane said, "Stacey, please sit down. We need to talk…"

The Interview

For the better part of two weeks, I had been mostly silent about the whole *incident*. My previous two press conferences were, to put it mildly, disasters. For the first one, I was so freaked out by all the cameras and people that I couldn't stand to be in the room for more than a few minutes.

The second one was so hostile that I stormed out of the room before it ever really began. Now, we would try it Traci's way. She had done all the preliminary work, the interviews with family and friends, with witnesses at the scene, with members of law enforcement; and now it was my turn.

We met the next day, she came to my room with a cameraman, and as he was setting up, she discussed the upcoming interview.

Traci started, "Now David, I am going to ask you some difficult questions, but don't worry, you can take your time answering.

"We can edit out any delay or hesitation that you might have. In addition, if you decide that you would like to change your response to any question, we can fix that too. It's important that you remain calm and composed; try not to think about the camera, just think of this as a conversation between two friends."

I nodded in agreement; the cameraman let Traci know that he was ready. She looked at me and smiled, "Are you ready?"

I nodded again. She gave the signal, and the cameraman began recording. Traci started the interview.

"I'm here with David Taylor, who until just recently, was an average everyday citizen going about his life in anonymity.

"That was until a fateful Saturday night when his life crashed headlong into five alleged criminals on a violent crime spree, culminating in a shootout that took the lives of four of the alleged criminals. David was seriously wounded, and I am told, is very lucky to still be alive.

"David, how are you feeling now?"

I shifted, uncomfortably, in my seat, "Well Traci, I am in a lot of pain."

Traci continued, "That's understandable. David, there has been a lot of speculation and rumor regarding your activities that night. Could you please tell me what you were doing that night before the shooting?"

Still trying to get comfortable in the seat, I addressed, "I was out with a few friends celebrating my thirtieth birthday."

Traci asked, "Who was with you?"

I replied, "I was with my good friend Chris and his wife, Lynn; also, there celebrating my birthday was another good friend, Terry."

Traci leaned in, ever so slightly, as she posited her next question.

"There was also another person present. Until yesterday her identity had not been established, but we now know that her name is Robyn Jenkins. Why would you try to hide her presence from the authorities and the press?"

I was still shifting about, trying to find that comfort level which had, thus far, eluded me, "Robyn was not supposed to be there."

Traci nodded, in anticipation for what was to come next.

"Why?"

"Robyn's husband does not think much of me," I had started to relax now, just a touch, "He would prefer that Robyn never speak to me again."

Ever the professional, Traci delved deeper into Robyn's involvement on that night.

"So, Robyn lied to her husband, to be with you; and then you and your friends tried to cover up her involvement so that her husband would not find out?"

I shrugged, "Yes."

Pushing farther, Traci continued, "Did Robyn plan on publicly acknowledging her involvement?"

That much sought-after confidence was starting to build inside of me.

"Yes, she did. However, before she could come forward, a videotape was released in which Robyn was identified."

Traci continued her line of questioning, "It has been speculated, by some, that you and Robyn are having an illicit affair. Is there any truth to this?"

With that confidence swelling inside my heart, I was now ready to answer the question.

"No, we are just friends. While it is true that at one time, we did date, we have not been romantically involved since before her wedding."

“It has also been alleged that you are the father of a twelve-year-old girl,” Changing topics, Traci inquired, “Is this a possibility?”

And just like that, my confidence had disappeared.

“Yes, it is. I did date the person who made the claim that I am her daughter’s biological father.”

“Were you aware of the child’s existence?’

I had started shifting about in my seat again.

“No. The last time I spoke with Jane, she told me directly that she was not pregnant.”

Traci persisted, “Then why would she claim that you were aware of the child all this time?”

Involuntarily, I shook my head in disbelief.

“I really don’t know. That is a question that you would need to ask her.”

Leaning forward again, Traci asked softly.

“If it is proven that you are indeed the biological father of this girl, what do you intend to do?”

I looked upward, for just a brief moment, because I could feel the emotion building up inside.

"I intend to become involved in her life. I would like joint custody; I would like to be the best father that I can be."

Changing topics again, Traci pondered— "Recently, there has been a vocal group of people calling you a racist. Are you a racist?"

A hint of anger swept across my face as I, emphatically, stated, "No. I do not believe that one race is better, or worse, than another."

Traci asked, "These same people have accused the Orlando Police Department, and Officer Rodriguez, in particular, of racial profiling. Do you think that racial profiling led to the eventual shootout that nearly cost you your life?"

That anger was beginning to flash in my eyes.

"No. If you are looking for a black male with dreadlocks, wearing a red jacket, then why would you not follow a person who fits that description?"

Traci presented her next question.

"Do you think that the police department, or Officer Rodriguez, could have done anything different that might have avoided this tragedy?"

"No," with teeth firmly clenched, I spit out, "Officer Rodriguez did not set this event in motion. The actions of five people started and, eventually, led to the tragic consequences of that night. Remember, Officer Rodriguez never fired a single shot, it was Calvin Jones who fired the first shot."

Sensing my agitation, Traci started her transition to the next topic.

"A lot of people consider you a hero for getting involved, and potentially saving the life of a police officer. Do you consider yourself a hero?"

Feeling that anger begin to dissipate, I reacted.

"No, I did what I hope anyone would do in the same situation."

Playing Devil's advocate, Traci continued her line of questioning.

"Others believe that the death of four young people, and the paralyzing of another, is too high a price to pay for the life of just one person. What do you say to these people?"

Firm in my conviction on this subject, I said, "A Police Officer puts his or her life on the line every time they report for duty. They protect us from the vilest of people, and I for one, value their lives more than that of any alleged thug, or criminal."

The journalist in Traci just could not help herself as she asked, "How much did you drink that night?"

Caught just a bit off guard, I replied, “I cannot comment at this time.”

Pushing just a little further, Traci continued, “Did that contribute to your actions?”

Resolute in my conviction, I stated— “I would like to think that impaired, or sober, I would have done the same thing.”

Switching topics again, Traci probed my opinions further.

“Currently there is legislation pending that would limit the types of guns available to the general public. Prior to the shooting were you a proponent of any gun control legislation?”

Once again, I shrugged.

“Honestly, I had never even thought seriously about it. I don’t own a gun; and I had no intention of owning a gun, so it didn’t matter to me if they did limit the availability of certain types of guns.”

Traci responded, “How do you feel about the gun control legislation now, after the shooting?”

I closed my eyes, for just a second or two, as I contemplated how to articulate my thoughts on the subject.

“I feel that the current legislation is inadequate. All the guns used by the alleged criminals were either stolen or otherwise illegally obtained. Ownership of a handgun, and the responsibility that comes with it, should be a privilege reserved for a select few."

Traci solicited, "What is next for you?"

I smiled, "I would like to go on about my life as before, but I know that's not possible."

Traci asked one last question, "Finally, who is David Taylor?"

Relieved that this interview was now over, I declared—"I am just an average guy who got caught up in an event that was much bigger than myself. I would hope that the world can accept this and allow me to move on with my life. I didn't ask for this to happen and I never wished for this happen. Please let it go away quietly."

Traci signaled for the cameraman to stop.

"That was great. You did a really wonderful job. Is there anything that you would like to change?"

Surprised by the passage of time, I replied, "No, I'm fairly happy with my responses. I didn't think that this would have been so easy for me."

Traci smiled, "I'm glad it went so well for you. After witnessing your press conferences, I wasn't sure how you would do, but I think that you handled yourself perfectly. I'll call you after the story airs to see what you think."

With the interview over, all Traci had to do was some editing before the scheduled airing later that evening. When the appointed time arrived, I switched on the television and waited for the interview to begin.

The special began with a recap of that Saturday night's events, featuring a timeline and introduction of the major players; special attention was given to the previous criminal records of the alleged criminals. The special went on to include an interview with my parents, Chris, Lynn, and then Terry.

Several witnesses were also interviewed, and then a handful of Orlando Police Officers were interviewed as well; some of their identities were concealed, and their voices altered, to protect their anonymity. The best-known videos of the incident were shown, and then my interview aired. Finally, the emotional interview of Officer Rodriguez's wife wrapped up the special.

It is a curious thing to see your story aired for the World to see. You never realize how much friends and family mean to you until you see their responses to your plight. It's also an odd thing, watching a complete stranger get so emotional when thanking you for doing something that seemed like the only logical course of action at the time. Odder still, is to see yourself on television answering questions that you never thought would have been asked prior to such an event.

When the show was over, the telephone rang. On the line was Traci.

"What did you think?"

I answered, "Wow, that was amazing!"

"Thank you. Let's see how people feel about you now." Traci stated with great satisfaction.

"How do we top this?" I asked.

"In a week or so, after the results of the DNA tests are available, we'll do another interview, one with Jane if it is necessary. Also, I would like to interview Robyn and get her side of the story."

"I won't push Robyn to allow an interview with you," I was still very concerned about the ramifications of such a request.

Traci countered, "You won't need to. She has to present her story sooner or later. I would prefer sooner."

"She doesn't have to say anything. I would prefer that she stay out of this."

"It's too late," Traci replied, "She has to make a statement; to the press and, eventually, to a jury if charges are filed."

"Still, I would rather Robyn not get involved with this thing."

"Why?" Traci asked, "Everyone now knows *who* she is; it doesn't make sense for her to try and avoid saying something."

I sighed, "Tom kicked her out of the house. That was the last thing that I wanted to happen."

"I'm sorry to hear that, but she needs to say something, publicly. I would like her to grant me the first interview."

"That's something you can discuss with her," I replied, "But I will not push her to make a statement."

"Do you mind if I call her and ask?"

I took in a deep breath and held it for a minute before I agreed to Traci's request.

"Sure, you can call her. Just don't expect her to agree to an interview."

A Little Give and Take

After Tom kicked Robyn out of the house, she settled on staying with her sister. Since Robyn and her sister generally did not get along anyway, it was a very difficult time for her. By now Robyn was no longer just answering her phone if she didn't recognize the number of the person calling; when her phone rang, she just let it go to voice mail. Afterwards, she called and checked her voice mail message; it was Traci Kaneko wanting to talk. She wrote down the number and called Traci back.

After a couple of rings, a familiar voice said, "Hello, this is Traci Kaneko. How can I help you?"

Robyn paused for a minute, before replying, "Hi, Traci, it's me, Robyn."

"Hi, Robyn," genuinely excited, Traci said, "David said it was alright if I called you to ask you a question. I'm in the process of putting together another special and I would like to include a segment on you. Would you be interested in granting me an exclusive interview?"

"Why would I do that?" Robin asked.

Traci responded, "Because, at some point, you will have to make a public statement. I would like the honor of presenting your story to the public. Listen, I know that David doesn't want you to get involved in all of this, but realistically it's too late for that. You have to make a statement and I would prefer it is with someone like me; a person that is trying to look after David and his public image."

Robyn considered her options, "What if I say no?"

"Then I won't bother you anymore about it," Traci replied.

Feeling cornered, Robyn asked, "And if I say yes, what type of questions do you plan on asking?"

Traci took a deep breath.

"I would have to ask you about your relationship with David. I would have to ask you why you were not honest with Tom about your relationship with David. I would definitely have to ask you what you were feeling as the shooting began. Granted, these will not be easy questions, but you will have to answer them publicly, at some point."

Very concerned about the subject matter, Robyn asked, "Do you think it would help David's public image?"

“It wouldn’t hurt it any, if that’s what you mean.”

Nearly a minute would go by before Robyn would answer, “I’ll do it…”

“That’s great!” a relieved Traci exclaimed, “When would you like to do the interview?”

“Any evening. I have lots of free time at night these days.”

“Okay, how about in two days?” Traci offered, “We can meet here at the station around eight, if that’s okay with you?”

“That’s fine. I’ll be there,” Robyn answered.

Traci said, “See you in two days.”

♦♦♦

Three days after the airing of Traci’s special, Rhonda Spears hit the airwaves with her own take on the events of that night. She interviewed the parents of William Baker and Marcus Porter, or the “victims”, as she liked to call them. Surprisingly, Theo Roberts was not interviewed; and other than his name and medical diagnosis, not much else was mentioned about him.

Also interviewed was the Mayor, the Chief of Police, and, of course, Detective Chris Welles had something to say as well. And yes, people from the neighborhood were also extremely critical of my actions, and they were not afraid to share their willingness to seek retribution. The fire and brimstone would be provided by Dr. Johnson.

After two minutes of unapologetic hatred cast in my direction, Rhonda began—

"Thank you, Dr. Johnson for gracing us with your presence tonight. Can you please explain why you are here in Orlando?"

Dr. Johnson replied in that distinctive over enunciation that he was known for, somewhere between a Southern drawl and a Harvard professor.

"Thank you for having me on tonight, Rhonda. I'm here to cast a light on the darkness that has befallen Orlando. I am, of course, referring to that racist perpetrator, David Alan Taylor, and his hateful actions on that Saturday night."

Rhonda continued, "You are referring to the incident that took the lives of four young men—"

"Four young, and virtuous, black men in the prime of their lives." Dr. Johnson interrupted, "And David Alan Taylor, that racist perpetrator, shot them down like *dogs* in the streets of Orlando."

Rhonda cleared her throat, leading up the big question she really wanted to ask.

"Dr. Johnson, do you believe that David Alan Taylor is a racist? Do you believe that David Alan Taylor is being protected from justice because of the color of his skin?"

"Of course, I do! The facts are, four young black men are dead, and the racist perpetrator who committed the crime still has not been charged with murder!"

"Yes, Dr. Johnson," Rhonda agreed, "This appears to be a travesty of justice. One that I hope the authorities will soon remedy."

Dr. Johnson responded, "It is my firm belief that justice will be served, and that racist perpetrator, David Alan Taylor, will spend the rest of his wretched life behind bars."

Rhonda concluded, "Thank you Dr. Johnson, for your valuable insight."

Dr. Johnson closed his dissertation with the following remarks, "Thank you, Rhonda. You are a true friend of black men and women, across this great country."

The much-anticipated interview with Tonya Jones, the grieving mother of Curtis and Calvin Jones, was scheduled to air after the obligatory commercials. Hey, everyone's got bills to pay; even a media organization intent on destroying the reputation of an innocent man. An innocent man who was just in the wrong place, at the wrong time, and now who was in way over his head. It would be the most damaging, and heart wrenching, moment of my life.

Rhonda began the interview, “Thank you, Mrs. Jones, for agreeing to this talk with me during this most difficult time.”

“Please, call me Tonya. And thank you for allowing me to talk about my sons…” Mrs. Jones voice trailed off as she began to intensely weep.

Rhonda reached out and lightly patted Tonya’s hand with her own.

“Tonya, it’s ok. Take your time.”

Tonya nodded as she regained some composure.

“My sons, Calvin and Curtis Jones.”

Rhonda continued, “Now Tonya, please tell us about your sons, Calvin and Curtis.”

Tonya wiped away the remaining tears with a handkerchief and smiled.

“My boys were everything to me…” Tonya’s expression visibly changed, from that brief moment of joy to one of intense sorrow, "until that man, that terrible man, shot my boys dead on the street."

Rhonda offered, "David Alan Taylor?"

Tonya nodded, "I can't even bring myself to say his name."

"That's perfectly understandable," Rhonda replied with disdain, "As a mother myself, I can't even imagine what you are going through right now. Is there anything that you would like to say to David Alan Taylor and the people who support his actions on that infamous night?"

Tonya nodded.

"How *dare* you! You killed my sons and then claim that you had no choice! That's a damn lie! You had plenty of choices, and you thought killing my sons was the best choice! And *shame* on you! All of you who support that terrible, racist man. All of you celebrating the deaths of my sons at the hands of that wicked white man—

"*You can all go to Hell!*"

Rhonda finished the interview.

"Compelling words, from a grieving mother. This is Rhonda Spears saying goodnight, America."

It almost made me hate myself; it was that powerful.

Meet Sean Walker

Thomas Patterson, the District Attorney responsible for the Orlando area, scheduled a press conference held the very next day. During the press conference a new face appeared back, and to the left, of Mr. Patterson. Eventually he would be introduced as Sean Walker, Assistant District Attorney, and lead prosecutor in the matter at hand.

As expected, Mr. Walker announced that a grand jury would be convened and that he would seek an indictment. Also present in the background, was that weasel Detective Chris Welles, with a stupid, smug look on his face. I knew that bastard would be at the press conference; there was no way that Welles, the egomaniac that he was, would miss a chance like this to pose in front of the cameras. As Mr. Walker droned on and on, the phone rang. On the line was Alice.

"Well, it's begun. Are you ready?"

Thoroughly engaged, I nodded to no one.

“Hi, Alice. I’m ready for anything. Are you watching this thing?”

“Yes, I am,” she replied.

“Did you see that asshole, Chris Welles?”

“Yes, I saw him.”

“What a dick!” I exclaimed.

“You’re very cheerful for someone who is facing an indictment.”

“Yeah, well Robyn has decided to move out of her sister’s house, and she is going to stay at my house,” I smiled at the thought.

“I don’t think that is wise…”

“It’s already done,” I cut her off, “Don’t try to talk me out of it.”

Alice sighed heavily, “You should have discussed this with me prior to making a decision like that. We have more than your love life to think about.”

“It’s not like that.”

Alice interjected, “Sure, and maybe someday you can explain this fascination with Robyn to me. Well, at least now we can go on the offensive.”

"What did you have in mind?"

Alice laughed, "You'll see."

♦♦♦

The next day, Alice held her own press conference. Surrounding her were several police officers in uniform. Nearly every department in the tri-county area was represented; this included members of the Orlando Police Department, Orange, Osceola, and Seminole Counties, as well as members of other cities in the area.

Alice began to speak— "Thank you ladies and gentlemen of the press for coming on such short notice. My name is Alice Miller, and I represent Mr. David Alan Taylor.

"Since the beginning of my involvement in this case, I have received several calls from members of our law enforcement community expressing their support of the actions taken by Mr. Taylor. All of the officers present today were willing to publicly show their support of Mr. Taylor, despite the repeated attempts of their superiors to discourage doing so. I had hoped that this press conference would not be necessary; however, the District Attorney's office has made it very clear that they intend to press charges. I also have someone here who would like to say a few words…"

As Alice turned and looked over her shoulder, the sea of Police Officers split to reveal Officer Paul Rodriguez, and his family. As they made their way to the microphone, the other Police Officers began to applaud. Officer Rodriguez, visibly emotional, adjusted the microphone and began to speak.

"My name is Paul Rodriguez, and this is my family. For those of you who do not know my name, I am the Officer who was shot in the back by Calvin Jones. It was the catalyst that set David's involvement with the events of that night into motion.

"A short time after the incident, my superiors went out of their way to inform me that if I spoke publicly about this incident, that I would lose my job as a Police Officer. After a series of discussions with my wife and family, we decided that, if necessary, we would come forward and support David Taylor.

"I am alive today…only because of the bravery, and the actions of David Taylor. I am forever in his debt, and I would rather find another line of work than let him become the victim of politics and politicians.

"Thank you, David, and God bless."

A thunderous round of applause erupted from the men and women in blue and, in some cases, green, as Officer Rodriguez and his family waved at the press and then disappeared.

Later that afternoon, Alice called to see what I thought about her press conference. I remember saying something to the effect of, *I'm glad you're on my side*.

I had grown tired of being the punching bag for Dr. James Johnson and Tonya Jones, and I wanted to start punching back. So, I sat down and wrote out my thoughts on a piece of paper. It was more or less the rambling sentences of a novice writer, touching on sensitive subjects such as racism and police profiling.

I was angry that I had become the target of hateful accusations, which showed in my letter. When I went back and read through it again, I was amazed at how wounded I really was by the actions of Dr. Johnson and Mrs. Jones. I knew that sentiment was not the real me, so I pitched that draft into the trash can and started all over again. The second letter came out much better.

Alice and I had discussed the option of written responses to the attacks of Dr. Johnson and Mrs. Jones. Yet, she wanted to edit anything that I wrote before being released to the public. So, I gave her a copy of the second letter; she took it back to her office to study and then make any necessary adjustments.

The following is what was sent to the newspaper:

Dear Editor: My name is Alice Miller, and I represent Mr. David Alan Taylor. Lately, Mr. Taylor has been the victim of a well-coordinated media assault denouncing his actions as racist in nature. The two primary perpetrators of this media smear campaign appear to be Dr. James Johnson and Mrs. Tonya Jones; these two people would have the world believe that my client set out that evening with the sole purpose of killing young black men. This simply is not true.

Mr. Taylor set out that evening to celebrate his 30th birthday with some close friends. It was unfortunate that Calvin Jones, Curtis Jones, William Baker, Marcus Porter, and Theo Roberts set out with something far more sinister in mind when they headed to downtown. They allegedly robbed an innocent man and woman at gunpoint, beating the man so severely that he almost died from his injuries.

As if that was not enough, these five young men [I do not refer to them as black men because color has no relevance in this case] attempted to elude the police, and ultimately shot Officer Paul Rodriguez in the back. The videotape and eyewitness accounts are very clear about who fired first and what happened next.

Mr. Taylor made a courageous decision to get involved and used a reasonable amount of force to prevent the death of Officer Rodriguez. From that point on, Mr. Taylor acted in self-defense, and with good reason. Mr. Taylor would eventually be shot three times, one bullet actually lodging behind his heart.

Dr. Johnson and Mrs. Jones would also have the world believe that these young men were fine outstanding gentlemen, pillars of their community. This also is not true. Most of these young men were either convicted felons or apparent suspects in felony offenses. These young men were alleged predators of the community, not misunderstood youths, as Dr. Johnson and Mrs. Jones have claimed.

Dr. Johnson and Mrs. Jones have also made a point of lamenting the loss of a 'good father', William Baker. In reality, William Baker had not seen his son in 18 months. William Baker also had refused to pay any child support.

I can understand how the grief of Mrs. Jones may have impaired her perspective in this matter. I do not understand why Dr. Johnson would embrace the half-truths and outright lies regarding the facts of this case.

Mr. Taylor is not now, nor has he ever been, a racist. And I should know, after all, I am a black woman who has personally seen the terrible effects of racism. I can confidently state that Mr. Taylor has treated me with the utmost respect and has never once made me feel like race was an issue.

Sincerely,

Alice Miller, Attorney

Home

Let me give you the 411 on surviving a media circus. There are two methods that are somewhat effective in evading the jackals commonly known as "Journalists".

First, there is the hide and seek method, where your lawyer has someone rent a secluded place in their name. Or the second method, hunker down and wait until the crisis passes.

Admittedly, it helps if you spend a couple of weeks in the hospital. This allows friends and family the time to pursue the 'hunker down' method. It also helps if you have someone willing to deceive the jackals, I mean, journalists, until you have left the hospital and are already home.

Thanks, Doc.

The next day I got the news that I had been waiting for since the beginning of this ordeal; I was informed that I would be released from the hospital the following day. Now, to this point, my parents have barely been mentioned in this story. During my stay in the hospital, my mom came by every day to check on me. She would always ask how I was doing and if I wanted to talk about what happened. However, as a thirty-year-old man, I found it difficult to discuss my anxieties with her. As a result, we would sit there and just look at one another and talk about the weather or other trivial things.

My dad would also come by at night, not every night, but most nights. Again, as a thirty-year-old man, I found it difficult to discuss my feelings regarding the gunfight with my father. Instead, we would talk about the *Dolphins*, the *Magic*, or any other sports team that would come to mind.

When it finally was time for me to leave the hospital, my parents were there to take me home. Now, I have always had a decent relationship with my parents, but I do not tell them everything. One of the things that I had failed to mention to them was the fact that Robyn would be staying with me. Imagine their surprise when Robyn opened the front door and came out to help me.

"What is *she* doing here?" my mother whispered in my ear.

I whispered back, "Mom, she's here because she has no other place to stay."

Now, my parents liked Robyn well enough when we were dating, but they were less than thrilled with our relationship now. After twenty or so awkward minutes, my parents left. Before they were gone, my mom asked me, "Are you sure that you want to stay here? You can always come stay at our house."

I muttered, *"Mom!"*

"I'm just saying that you might be more comfortable at our house."

I responded, "I'll be just fine. Will you quit worrying about me; I am thirty years-old now."

"I know, but you'll always be my little baby," she replied.

"Mom! Go home," exasperated, I said, "I'll talk to you later."

Away they went; it was now just Robyn and me, finally.

♦♦♦

I was scheduled to attend my first physical therapy session in three days. I had only asked a handful of people for permission to be quoted in this book. My physical therapist was the only one to decline a record of our conversations about the racial divide in America, and how to reconcile our past with our future.

When I asked why, he simply replied, "This is your story, not mine."

I asked if I could at least pay tribute to his dedication, acknowledge our many conversations, and to honor our friendship, he said, "Sure."

So, here's to Randall Quinn, born on the Southside of Chicago, the son of a Tuskegee Airman and a Wisconsin farmer. Randall—don't *ever* make the mistake of calling him Randy—is a brother, a father, a husband, and one of my dearest friends, thank you for everything that you have done for me. Pain and torture may be your trade, but the lessons you have taught me, and the conversations we have had, will forever be a part of my life. Funny how life places you where you need to be.

Yes, the irony of that last sentence is not lost on me. I may be an idiot, but I'm not stupid. Perhaps someday, Randall will tell the story of his remarkable life, and, if deemed worthy enough, of our conversations. The world would be a much better place if this were Randall's story, not mine.

Oh, and Randall if you are reading this, Sasquatch in a thong is an actual thing. I saw it on the back of a book cover once. Look it up, I had to.

Congratulations, it's a 12-Year-Old Girl

A few days later, I got the call that I had been waiting for since Jane's surprise declaration. It was Alice on the phone, "I have the results of the DNA test."

My emotions elevated as I asked, "Tell me, am I a father or not?"

"Congratulations, it's a twelve-year-old girl," Alice stated.

"I'm a father?"

"Yes, you are," Alice replied.

I actually dropped the phone and began crying. I could hear Alice on the other end, asking if I was alright. I picked the phone back up, trying to hold back the tears, and said, "I'm okay. Can I call Jane now?"

Alice answered, "You're too emotional right now. Let me call her."

No longer rational, I implored, “No. I need to talk to her.”

“I think it would be better if I called Jane,” Alice insisted.

Still fighting logic, I demanded, “No, I can handle this. I need to talk to her at some point anyway.”

I picked up the phone and dialed Jane’s number. After a couple of rings, a familiar, but hesitant voice answered.

“Hello?”

Completely overwhelmed by the situation, I said, “Hello Jane, it’s me, David.”

“Hello David,” Jane paused for a moment before continuing, “I’m so sorry.”

“You should be. We have the results of the DNA tests…”

“…and you are the father,” Jane completed my sentence.

“Yes,” I replied.

“I know. David, I’m so sorry that I didn’t tell you when you called back then. I was angry and hurt and I didn’t want you to be involved in my life. If I could go back in time and change things I would.”

“I know,” I reluctantly acknowledged her apology.

“Are you angry at me?” Jane asked.

In a moment of fairness, I reflected on our relationship at that time. We were both so young, so naive to how the world really works. I decided that I was just as much to blame for this debacle as Jane, but I just didn't know how to express it out loud.

"Jane, I honestly don't know what to think. I've missed so much of Stacey's life, so many things that I would have wanted to experience as a father."

"I wouldn't blame you if you are angry," Jane added.

I responded, "What about the interview you did? Why would you lie like that?"

"I did it because Rhonda Spears told me to," Jane started to cry, "She said it would be easier to explain to Stacey that you were an uninterested father rather than tell her the truth."

I winced, in emotional pain.

"Jane, you made me look really bad. I can't afford to look bad right now."

Jane apologized, "I know, I'm sorry. If there is anything that I can do to make it up to you, please let me know."

Bluntly, without any consideration of how it would sound, I said, "Yeah, you can tell the truth."

“I can do that. David, would you like to speak to your daughter?” Jane asked.

I said, “I’m not ready for that yet.”

A subdued Jane replied, “I understand. When would you like to speak to Stacey?”

I asked, “Does she know the truth yet?”

Jane replied, “Yes, David. I told her just after I got the letter from your lawyer.”

I said, “Give me a day or two please.”

I went on to say my goodbyes. I immediately headed for the liquor cabinet; I needed a drink in the worst possible way. I poured a very tall glass of rum and added a splash of cola for color. I sucked it down, and then made another.

Yeah, it was going to be a long night.

Yeah, That Happened…

Traci had finally pieced together her next special. This one featured interviews with Alice, Robyn, Officer Rodriguez, Terry, Chris, and my parents. The first interview was with Alice. Alice laid out our primary defense; that I only got involved after Calvin Jones had shot Officer Rodriguez in the back. Alice continued to state that I had used a justifiable amount of force to save the life of Officer Rodriguez and that I was in fear of my own life when I shot the remaining suspects. She reiterated that this shooting was not racially motivated, as some people had charged.

Alice also stated that she believed my possible prosecution was based on political considerations, and not on the legality of the shooting. She stressed the Florida law allowing the use of deadly force to protect another person, or oneself, from bodily harm. She attacked the City of Orlando leadership, including the Mayor and the Chief of Police, for caving into the pressure applied by special interest groups seeking retribution for my actions.

The next interview was with Chris. He portrayed me as a sensitive, do anything for a friend kind of guy. He also stressed that I was, in no way, a racist. Chris said he felt I did the right thing, and hoped he would have done the same, under the circumstances. Chris finished by questioning the logic behind the District Attorney's seemingly overzealous response to the shooting, and he wondered why the city leaders appeared to be so adamant about pushing for the prosecution of me.

Next up was Terry. He also discussed our past, how long we had known each other, and why he waited for so long before coming forward and admitting the truth about what happened that night. Terry also confirmed his belief that I did do the right thing and finished by questioning the decision of the city leadership to pursue criminal charges.

The next interview was with my parents. It was the first time that they had publicly commented on the *incident*. My Mother cried as she talked about when they first heard about the shooting. They talked about visiting the hospital, and how I looked with all those tubes and wires surrounding me. They talked about my childhood, my schooling, and the sports that I played. They stressed their support of me and talked about my life after the incident. When asked if they had anything to say to my detractors, they responded with a *how dare you question our son's intentions*. They said that they were sorry for the loss of life, but that I absolutely did the right thing.

Now came the interview that everyone was waiting for, the interview with Robyn. She talked candidly about our relationship, both past and present. She spoke about how we first met, and what led up to the events of that night. She discussed her desire to come forward, and my desire to protect her from the media and the authorities.

She also talked about her marriage, and the aftereffects of the *incident*. She continued, expressing her admiration of my actions, and admitted to caring a great deal about my well-being. She ended her interview by voicing her support of me and chastising the city of Orlando for being overly concerned about the political ramifications of the *incident*.

The final interview of the special was with Officer Paul Rodriguez, and his family. He talked about what was going through his mind as he followed the suspects. He explained how it felt to be shot in the back, the subsequent pain, confusion, and ultimately his regaining of consciousness prior to the arrival of the ambulances. He recalled the conversation he had with his superiors, who threatened to fire him if he spoke publicly about the *incident*. He reminisced about the discussions with his wife and family, and his desire to support me publicly despite any subsequent repercussions. He talked about the accusations of racial profiling and finished by stressing his desire to remain a police officer.

The next afternoon, the phone rang. On the line was Jane.

"Are you ready to talk to your daughter?"

I swallowed a major lump, as I said, "Yeah, I think so."

The next voice I heard was Stacey's.

"Hello David, it's me, Stacey; or would you prefer that I call you Dad?"

Something inside of me retreated, "You can call me anything you like. How are you?"

"I'm fine. How are you?"

"I'm a wreck," I admitted, "I don't know what to say…"

Stacey answered, "It's okay. My mom already told me that you didn't know about me."

Trying to hold back the tears at this point in the conversation, I said, "I'm so sorry. I wish I had been there for you. I feel terrible…"

"It wasn't your fault. Mom lied to you; she lied to me too…" Stacey whispered to me.

"Don't blame your mother. I hurt her; she was very young then, and she made a tough decision. It was my fault—"

"No, it wasn't," interrupting me, Stacey corrected.

"Let's just say that it was a misunderstanding," I added, "I hope that we can get past this."

Changing the subject, Stacey asked, "Do you want to see me?"

I smiled, "Of course I do."

"When?" Stacey asked excitedly.

"That's something your mom and I need to work out."

Stacey replied, "My mom says that you live in Orlando."

"Yes. Yes, I do," I tried my best to stay calm, but fear was gnawing away at my resolve.

Stacey asked, "Can we go to Disney? If we go there?"

Trying to hide my discomfort, I laughed, "Of course, we can. Can I talk to your mom now?"

Ending our first conversation together, Stacey said, "Yeah. Goodbye…"

Emotionally wounded, I said, "Goodbye Stacey, I'll talk to you soon."

Jane got back on the phone.

"Yes David?" I could no longer keep my composure; I began crying uncontrollably, "David are you okay?"

In between sobs, I said, "No, I'm not. I can't believe that this is happening to me."

Apologizing again, Jane said, "David, I'm so sorry…"

Shaking my head, I uttered, "Listen Jane, I would like to meet Stacey as soon as possible."

"Do you want us to go there? Or would you like to come up here?"

In my mind, everything began to spin, "I really can't travel right now, so you would need to come here."

"When do you want to do this?" Jane asked with what seemed like genuine empathy to my emotional breakdown.

To my surprise, I repeated, "As soon as possible."

"Okay," Jane replied, "Do you want me to make the arrangements, or do you want to make the arrangements?"

"You make them," I declared, "and I'll pay for it. I want you to be able to come when it is convenient for you."

Jane said, “Okay. I’ll call you when I have the time and date set.”

Still crying, I said, “Fine. Goodbye, Jane.”

“Goodbye, David,” Jane ended our conversation.

Again, I headed to the liquor cabinet; I pulled out the rum and made a good stiff drink. I drank it down and then made another; it was going to be another long night.

David, Meet Your Daughter

One of the most frequent questions that I am asked is, how did I avoid the press? Well, at this point, I was not driving at all. No one would ever enter, or exit, a vehicle if the garage door was open. And the cars that Robyn and Terry drove each had newly installed dark limousine tint, making it nearly impossible to see inside said vehicle. So, often I would hide in the back seat until we were a safe distance from the house and then emerge from the floorboard of the car that I was riding in at the time.

In addition, we kept the blinds closed and the screen for my pool enclosure had been completely covered in tarps, so no one could see into the house, or even the backyard. It made for a weird look around the pool, but it was very effective in keeping out the prying eyes of the press. As a result, the press was never really sure if I was ever home, or not, and, in those early days, I was, mostly, not home.

I spent a great of time at Terry's house, it was my escape from the everyday stress caused by the presence of the press. We knew that, eventually, the press would lose interest and go away; all we had to do was just wait them out. Another bigger story would soon take my place, it truly was just a matter of time, and, at that point, I had plenty of time to wait it out.

Another trick that we used involved an “anonymous” tip to the press that I had been spotted somewhere in public. The news vans would pack up and go, and then we could have some peace and quiet, at least for a little while. I say this now to explain how we accomplished what happened next.

The following afternoon, Jane called me again. She had made the necessary travel arrangements; she and Stacey would be arriving in Orlando next Tuesday afternoon. I told Jane that I could mail her a check or give her the airfare upon arrival. She said that it wasn’t necessary to pay her back, but I insisted that I would. She relented and said that I could pay her back when I saw her. I offered to let them stay at my house, but Jane thought it would be better if they stayed in a nearby hotel. I didn’t object; it certainly made more sense than my offer (what with the media circus camped outside most of the time) and then we said our goodbyes.

I had to plan for someone to pick up Jane and Stacey. I called Terry and asked if he could pick them up from the airport. He said that he would rearrange his schedule. With that done, I started drinking again. It was becoming a bad habit of mine, but considering the stress I was under, it was surprising that I wasn't drinking more.

♦♦♦

The days seemed to disappear, and suddenly it was next Tuesday. Terry called me to tell me they had arrived on time and that he had just dropped them off at the hotel. I was already drinking when he called, so I invited him over for a drink. He said that he would stop by, and he was there in a few minutes. I poured him a drink and we sat down before I asked him about Stacey.

He said that she was a beautiful girl, and, clearly, she must have gotten it from her mother. We laughed for a while, like good friends do when they get together. Terry told me that Jane and Stacey would meet me the next morning.

After Robyn got home, she started drinking with us, and the three of us stayed up well into the middle of the night. Terry decided that it was way too late to go home, so he stayed at my house in my other spare bedroom.

The next morning, I got a call from Jane. She, and Stacey, were ready to see me now. I shook Terry back to life and ensured he was ready to pick Jane and Stacey from the hotel.

Quite by coincidence, an "anonymous" tipster had spotted me in a local park. The news vans rolled away as if on cue and left their precious vigil.

Robyn drove me directly to Terry's house. Shortly after, Terry left to pick Jane and Stacey up from the hotel. Robyn quietly dropped me off and then headed back to my house to keep up the well-coordinated subterfuge. Terry randomly drove around for fifteen minutes or so, before actually heading to the hotel. This afforded Robyn the necessary time to make her secret delivery and then start the journey back to the house.

Once safely inside Terry's home, I tried my best to make myself emotionally ready for what was about to happen. I had time to prepare myself for the moment, but I knew that I wasn't really ready for this. Yet, here I was, waiting to face my past. I could hear the garage door open. Ready or not; it was time to meet my daughter.

I opened the door and there before me were Jane and Stacey. Jane had not changed much since I saw her last, but my attention was entirely focused on Stacey. Although I had never seen her before, I would have recognized her anywhere.

Jane spoke first, "David, meet your daughter, Stacey."

"Hi…" I didn't know what else to say.

The butterflies inside of me soon gave way to the bees who, in turn, ceded control to the yellow jackets. I was simultaneously scared, nervous, angry, and truly humbled by this moment. It's the little things in life that make a difference, and this was, perhaps, the biggest little thing that I had ever done. And, of all the little things that I had done in my life, I would really like to have that one moment in time back, again. You see, I was so intent on finding a deeper meaning in this moment that I was completely oblivious to Jane and Stacey waiting for an invitation to enter the house.

Jane eventually asked, "Can we come in?"

"Please do, I'm sorry," I replied as I struggled to hold in the sea of emotions I was experiencing at the time.

As they walked into Terry's house, I found myself looking at Stacey and trying to figure out what traits, if any, came from me. At first glance, I didn't see any, Stacey looked exactly like her mother; however, as I looked closer, I saw something familiar. I made a mental comparison to me at her age, and I realized that we shared subtle similarities around the eyes and nose. I also noticed that her hair color was the same as mine when I was her age.

I was still having a hard time fighting back the tears of three distinct emotions: joy, sorrow, and regret. Joy because I was a father, sorrow because I had missed so much of her life, and regret because I had missed so many important milestones that I could never recreate. My emotional distress was obvious to Jane.

"It's all right David," she whispered in my ear, "Take a deep breath. You can't make up twelve years in a few minutes. Just start by saying hello to your daughter."

After a couple of deep breaths, and a hard swallow to vanquish that huge lump in my throat, I managed to say, "Hello Stacey."

I could tell that Stacey was experiencing her own version of my anxiety. She fidgeted around looking, first at the ground, and then at me.

"Hello," her voice was slightly different in person. It was, somehow, softer than I remembered from our conversation on the phone.

Okay that wasn't so bad, but now what? I could hear myself starting to play the *'What If'* game in my head. I was lost, and Jane could see it in my eyes.

Again, Jane leaned over and said, "Talk to her. She won't bite."

After a couple of more deep breaths and another hard swallow, I said, “So Stacey how was your flight?”

“It was okay.”

“Have you been on a plane before?” I mentally kicked myself for asking such a stupid question.

Stacey hesitated, as if she were deep in thought, and then abruptly said, “Yeah.”

My mind was going blank; there were a million things that I wanted to ask. I had rehearsed what I wanted to say, and now, I couldn’t think of a single thing. Then, somewhere among all of the important questions to ask, I came up with— “Do you like video games?”

That got her attention. Enthusiastically Stacey said, “Yeah!”

“Over there by the TV is Terry’s video game collection. Why don’t you go play some games while I talk to your mother?”

Stacey didn’t even wait for me to finish; she was already on the way to the console. I let out a sigh of relief as Jane and I sat down. Jane started, “David, you’re making this way too hard.”

I looked her in the eyes and said, “I know, but this is my first experience with being a father. I don’t know what to do.”

I could feel that lump again, fighting its way back up my throat.

“You’re doing fine,” Jane smiled.

While Stacey was occupied with Terry’s video game collection, Jane caught me up on twelve years of Stacey’s life. She showed me various pictures of Stacey, starting from when she was a baby, up until just last week. She explained that Stacey was an excellent student, consistently earning A’s and B’s on her report cards. Stacey enjoyed playing sports, especially soccer, and she was also very outgoing with lots of friends.

I told Jane that she had done an excellent job raising our daughter. It sounded funny saying our daughter, but it just felt so right in my heart. I could feel myself swelling with pride.

After a couple of hours, our first meeting was over. I had spent most of the time talking to Jane, but I had met my daughter. For me, it was one of the best days of my life. Jane and I decided that we would get together again and then go to *Disney*. They were only in town for four more days and we had to get as much done as possible.

We set up a game plan. The next day, Jane and Stacey would go shopping together during the day, and that night they would come over for dinner. The day after, we would all go to *Disney* and then on their final day we would spend it at Terry's house.

The next four days went by so quickly. As each minute passed, I grew more comfortable with being a Dad. It touched my heart so much watching Stacey running around *Disney*. The next day, Robyn and Terry joined us for a cookout. We grilled hamburgers and hot dogs; Stacey even helped me man the grill.

When it was time for Jane and Stacey to go, I rode with Terry while he took them to the airport. When we arrived, Terry helped Jane get their luggage out and over to a Sky Cap. Jane and I said our goodbyes, and now it was time to say goodbye to Stacey.

She came up and gave me a hug; it was the first hug that I had gotten from Stacey during her stay in Orlando. I could feel tears rolling down my face, as that pride swelled in my heart, "Goodbye Stacey," I whispered somberly as I kissed her on the forehead.

"Goodbye," she said, and then she kissed me on the cheek.

As they walked away, I found myself coaxing out a barely audible, “Stacey, I love you.”

Stacey looked back as if she heard me. She smiled and waved at me; and then they disappeared into the airport.

Terry and I headed straight back to the house and began another serious bout of drinking. Eventually, Robyn came home and the three of us drank well into the middle of the night.

The Fallout of an Indictment

Three days later, I got a call from Alice.

"David," she said, "My sources tell me that they are going to announce your indictment within forty-eight hours. It is important that we plan to turn you in to the authorities, and then bail you out, when the time comes."

I didn't want to think about it, I had enough on my mind.

"Can we talk about this later?"

Alice stressed, "No, David. We need to discuss this now."

I relented, "Okay. What do we do?"

"I have already spoken with the District Attorney's office." Alice sympathetically responded, "When you are indicted, they will allow you twenty-four hours to turn yourself in. Once you are processed, there will be a hearing to determine the amount required to bail you out of jail. The District Attorney will ask for a very high amount, perhaps five-hundred-thousand, or more. I will request that you be released on your own recognizance.

"The judge will probably decide on an amount somewhere between the two. I have received a pledge to cover your bail, but it may take a little time to put it together. Any time you spend in jail will be isolated from the general population."

"Great!" Alice could hear the sarcasm in my voice.

"Don't worry about this David." Alice soothed, "We knew this would happen. We will get through this..."

Resigned to my fate, I responded, "Just get me out as soon as you can."

"I will. Get some rest, David. You're going to need it."

♦♦♦

As promised, Sean Walker held a press conference the next day. He announced my indictment for four counts of second-degree murder, two counts of attempted murder. Oh, I bet you forgot about Peter Watson, didn't you? I know that I did. Plus, eight counts of discharging a firearm within city limits.

As promised, I turned myself in to the authorities. I was processed and held for a few hours in isolation as Alice worked to secure my release on bond. Surprisingly, the district

Attorney's office only requested a $100,000 bond. Alice worked her magic and the judge decided on a $50,000 bail. Within six hours of my incarceration, I was once again on my way home.

Although I know that I had received special treatment, it still was a nerve-wracking experience. Once I got home, I headed straight for the liquor cabinet. Clearly my drinking was becoming a problem, however, after the day that I just had, I could go one more day without confronting the issue.

The next day, I started drinking early. After a couple of drinks, the phone rang. It was my boss, Brenda. Up until this point, work had been very supportive, but now I was hearing a different story. It seems my employer had decided that, since the announcement of my indictment and future prosecution, I had become a liability. Therefore, it would be in the best interest of all involved if I would just resign.

I told her, *'Hell no, I won't resign!'* and went on to suggest that she contact my lawyer. She felt it was unnecessary to involve my lawyer and went on to imply that if I did not resign now, she would be forced to fire me. She said that if I were to resign, then I would receive one year of salary and medical coverage. If I did not resign, and was fired, then I would receive nothing.

"We will see what my attorney has to say!" I responded harshly, and then hung up the phone.

I called Alice and told her what had happened; she was pissed. Alice asked me if I really wanted to stay at my job, or would I be interested in leaving. I told her that I didn't want to go back to work anyway, but I still needed a paycheck until this thing was over. Alice assured me that she would handle the problem.

After she got off the phone with me, Alice called Brenda and demanded an explanation. Brenda protested Alice's involvement, but not before offering one year's severance pay and medical coverage again. Alice was insulted by the offer and threatened to mention my company's name at every single press conference until further notice. Brenda responded by saying the company would offer me an additional month for every year I had been employed, amounting to an additional seven months of severance and benefits.

Alice countered with a minimum of two-year severance, including medical coverage, explaining that it would be the only way to assure my quiet exit from the company. The company, and Brenda reluctantly agreed, provided that I would not publicly mention said company by name.

It was agreed that, if asked, I would refer to the company as a leader in the

telecommunications industry. The paperwork would be drawn up and mailed as soon as possible for Alice's review. Alice called me back and gave me the news; I was ecstatic.

Yet, I didn't have a lot of time to dwell on my indictment; Jane and I had decided to work out the details of joint custody as soon as possible. Two days after my release from jail, I was sitting in Alice's office on a conference call with Jane, Alice, and the arbitrator. Fortunately, there were no major stumbling blocks to reaching an agreement, and two hours later we had an accord. All that was left to do was type up the arrangement, sign it, and then submit it to the court.

Due to Jane's admission that she misled me about Stacey, Jane was not seeking and did not receive any back child support. I did promise to begin paying $500 a month in child support, beginning immediately after our agreement was legally accepted. We agreed it would be in the best interest of Stacey that, during the school year, except for holidays, that I would travel to New York for any visitation.

During the summer, Stacey would be allowed to stay with me for at least one month and, whenever possible, Jane and I would alternate holidays. We also agreed that I would be allowed to contact Stacey whenever I wanted, and more importantly, Stacey could contact me whenever she wanted. It was also determined that Jane would continue to provide medical and dental insurance. At the same time, I would pay half of any deductibles or additional related charges. Overall, I think it was a very fair and amicable deal for all parties involved.

With the arbitration out of the way, it was time for Alice and me to hit the figurative road; it was time to hit the talk show circuit. We did network interviews, local interviews, radio, and cable news. We had a lot of ground to make up since our main adversaries, Dr. Johnson and Mrs. Jones had been hard at work spreading their version of that night's events.

On almost a daily basis since the *incident*, Dr. Johnson and Tonya Jones had been hammering away at my intentions. Mrs. Jones' anger and Dr. Johnson's public relations skills were a formidable combination. Always bordering on slander, the "dastardly duo", as I liked to call them, seemed to have the world believing that I was a 'racist'.

Yes, we had some work to do, but Alice was brilliant.

Contrary to what you might think, life on the talk show circuit isn't all that bad. Most of the interviews we did were on somebody else's dime; we traveled for free, we ate for free, and we stayed in nice hotels, for free. The worst part for me was the waiting to appear on the public airwaves. I still had not gotten over my fear of cameras, or public speaking. Thankfully, Alice did most of the talking.

Someone once told me, if you do something uncomfortable for long enough, you will find a way to make it comfortable. That someone was my speech teacher in college; a class I escaped with the only *'D'* of my collegiate career. But wouldn't you know it, she was right; I did find a way to make myself more comfortable before the press. Three parts vodka and one-part orange juice; drink and repeat as necessary. Throw in a couple of breath mints and I was good to go. Alice didn't know about my pre-interview ritual; she just thought I was adjusting to life in the spotlight.

It's Official: You're a Dad (Now What Do I Do?)

It took about a month for all the paperwork to be processed, and then submitted for approval. By this time, Alice and I were well into our press junket. Within days of receiving the paperwork, the presiding judge made it official. We had arrived at the next hotel, and I was sleeping when I got a call from Alice, she said, "It's official; you're a Dad."

That lump was back in my throat again. I remember thinking to myself, '*Now what do I do?*'

I got off the phone with Alice and called Jane. We spoke for a while about my official status as a Dad. Then I spoke with Stacey, she was all excited knowing that she really had a Dad. We also talked about school and what she was doing in class. Stacey confided in me that she was already making plans for the summer, where she wanted to go, and what she wanted to do.

Stacey wasn't saying I love you yet, but she did say that she missed me.

It was a start, and a good excuse to start drinking again when I got off the phone.

♦♦♦

Preparation for the upcoming trial began the following week. Alice had several individual and group meetings with everyone involved. She staged mock trails, simulating the anticipated cross-examinations of the Assistant District Attorney. Alice covered everyone's history and learned what, if anything, might be brought up in trial by the prosecution. For some of us, the list was quite long. After one of these marathon sessions Alice decided it was time for me to tell her all about my past. I responded with, "What do you want to know?"

"I know that you and Chris are close friends from school, but I need to know why you are so close."

I laughed, "Well, growing up there was a group of us that hung out together; it was kind of like a loosely organized gang. It was rare for everyone to be present at the same time, but there were four of us who always seemed to be in the middle of everything: Kevin, James, Chris, and myself.

"The four of us were always together; Kevin and James were the more outgoing and flamboyant members of our group. Chris was the most popular one though; it seemed as if everyone knew who he was. Chris was also a talented musician, a good-looking guy, and an all-around great person.

"I, on the other hand, was the quiet one of the group. I was the guy that people would always see, but few knew my name. To everyone that we met, I was the mysterious, silent stranger. People would always make assumptions about me, and they would fill in the gaps of my life with their imaginations. What people dreamed up about me was way more interesting than the actual truth. I was then, and I continue to be, a shy person.

"As our reputations grew, so did our egos, with the notable exception of Chris. No matter how popular Chris was, he remained a humble person. It wasn't long before Kevin, James, and I were showing signs of spiraling out of control. We were all doing a bunch of stupid things, but, surprisingly, we somehow managed to avoid disaster, legally or otherwise. I had developed a nasty reputation as a womanizer, someone who would do, or say anything to get what I wanted.

"I crossed a lot of lines, and offended many people, but for some reason no one ever stopped me. I kept pushing the limits trying to find out how far I could go; the only thing that kept me somewhat grounded in reality was Chris. He was one of the few people who would ever, candidly, tell me when I had gone too far, and because I respected him, his opinion meant a great deal to me.

"Although we don't see each other much anymore, I still value his opinions. His personality hasn't changed at all over the years; to this day he remains a humble person who would do anything for a friend. Knowing Chris makes me want to be a better person."

"What about Terry?" Alice asked.

Again, I laughed, "Terry and I met about eight years ago, when we both worked for the same company. Terry and I are a lot alike, but we are like night and day when it comes to personality. He is very outgoing, while I am not.

"We have similar likes, and dislikes, and enjoy many of the same hobbies. Professionally Terry has always done better than me, but it's hard to be in sales and sales management when you are a shy person. We both enjoy hanging out with good friends, sports, and drinking.

"Over the years, Terry and I have been there for one another as life threw its share of curve balls in our direction.

With each incident our friendship grew and grew, today we are more like brothers than friends."

Alice continued, "Now comes the big question, what is the obsession with Robyn?"

I had stopped laughing.

"Robyn and I met at a record store. I was the Assistant Manager, and she was a customer. The first time I saw Robyn, she had just walked in the front door with her brother. For me, it was love at first sight. There was just something about her that made me turn to jelly inside.

"That day I asked her if she would be interested in registering for a contest we were running, she filled out the form, which included such information as her name, age, and phone number. What she didn't know was that I never turned in her form; I kept it for myself. I just wanted to know her name.

"Over the next few weeks, it was understood by the other record store employees that I was the only one who could help Robyn. It didn't matter where I was in the store, or what I was doing at the time— when they saw her coming in, they would find me. We would flirt with one another, and, eventually, I asked her if she would like to go out sometime. We agreed to meet at Visage, the hottest nightclub in town for people like us.

“After closing the record store that night, Kevin, James, Chris, and I started drinking before we even headed to Visage. By the time we got to there, I had a really good buzz going. I walked in the door and immediately started looking for Robyn; eventually I found her on the dance floor. As she was dancing, I walked up behind her when, just as I reached her, she turned around. Without saying a word, I stepped up and kissed her; long, passionate, and hard. When I was done, I turned and walked away; it was one of the most defining moments of my life.

“I remember that feeling bubbling up inside when I spotted her on the dance floor. The hope, the desire, the love that I felt as I made my way toward her. She was like a Siren drawing me closer and closer to the jagged rocks. And I would willingly go to a certain death, if just to feel her touch. I know it was so many years ago, but I still feel that when I look at Robyn today. I just don’t act on it anymore.

“Within a few days, Robyn invited me to spend the night at the beach with her. That night we walked along the dark beach, hand in hand. As we walked, I told her everything about me, including all the bad things that I had ever done. It wasn’t long before I was professing my love to Robyn, and to my delight, she admitted that she loved me too.

"Robyn is the only person that I have never ever lied to, about anything. Well, except for you, Terry, Traci, and now Stacey. Ours was a storybook romance, and yet fate had conspired to keep us apart."

Alice, genuinely intrigued, asked, "What happened?"

I sighed, "Robyn and Tom were in the slow painful process of breaking up when Robyn and I met. To his credit, Tom hung in there and was able to eventually work things out with Robyn. During that period of their relationship, Robyn would break up with me only to come back again.

"This was okay with me because all I really wanted to do was be with Robyn, everything else was just icing on the cake. At some point though, Robyn had to choose between Tom and me. She chose Tom, and two years later they got married.

"I have always respected her decision, but our deep emotional connection keeps us together. We have gone months, years even, without speaking, but in the end, we would find each other again. And now our deep emotional connection has again driven a wedge between Robyn and Tom."

"What about Jane?" Alice delved deeper into my personal life.

I smiled.

“Jane and I met a couple of years earlier. There was an instant mutual attraction, and it didn’t take long before we were dating. Things were going fine, but then I screwed up. I cheated on Jane, and she found out.

“It was a messy break up; and a couple months later her dad got a work promotion, which led to her moving to New York. During the breakup, Jane told me that she was pregnant and wanted money for an abortion. I told her to come and get the money; but she never did.

“After she moved, I heard rumors that she was, indeed, pregnant. I got her phone number from a mutual friend and called her to find out if the rumors were true. Jane insisted that she was not pregnant and asked that I did not contact her again. I thought the matter was resolved, but here I am, a Dad.”

Alice felt that we had covered enough for the day. After years of trying to avoid the emotions, Alice had forced me to confront my past. It definitely called for another night of serious drinking, maybe then I could bury my past again.

A Little Good News & A Lot of Bad News

Dr. Johnson and Tonya Jones were at it again; this time the dastardly duo was attacking Alice Miller. It's crazy, but the two of them were publicly questioning Alice's *"blackness"* as they phrased it. They reasoned that Alice had forsaken her ancestry because she was representing me in the upcoming trial.

They explained that anyone who respected their black heritage would not, in good conscience, represent a racial killer like me. They went on to question Alice's ethics, legal experience, and character. To me, and, more importantly, to Alice, it came across as one more desperate attempt to racially polarize the community.

The day after Dr. Johnson and Tonya Jones aired their allegations, Alice received an unexpected call. Theo Roberts was on the line, expressing his desire to publicly support my actions that night. It seems that, since the incident, Theo had gone through all the stages of grief regarding his injuries, and, at some point during the process, he had accepted God. He felt it was his responsibility to defend my actions that night. This was a major development for my defense; imagine the impact of the only survivor wanting to support me.

The president of a certain national gun rights lobbying group (remember that silly lawsuit) was frustrated. Despite his covert efforts to derail public support for me, the polls clearly showed a positive trend. It was painfully evident that biased media coverage and racism accusations just weren't enough to achieve the desired effect. An all-out frontal assault seemed to be the next logical step. The proper timing of such an attack, however, would be necessary. He would not have to wait long for the perfect opportunity.

A local small-time, weekly magazine would print an article that would send shockwaves through the members of that still unnamed national gun-lobbying group. The article was, to say the least, very anti-gun. Firmly a liberal-leaning magazine, this dogma was nothing new. But the quote attributed to a close associate of mine, and reputed to be my very words, was new. According to the magazine I supposedly said, and strictly for legal purposes, I am quoting the magazine:

"The NRA is made up of a bunch of fucking idiots, who would sell their own mother in order to carry a gun into church."

Now, in all honesty, I never said that. I may have thought it, but I *never* said it. To make matters worse, the magazine did not, and would not identify the source of this "heinous" (think lawsuit) statement. Within days, the hate mail started coming in. In a little more than a week, I suddenly found myself slapped with a libel lawsuit and facing an outraged and vocal president.

He was spewing fire and brimstone, applauding his organization's mission, and simultaneously beating the hell out of me. He was determined and organized; utilizing all forms of media: newspapers, TV news, talk shows, magazine articles, web blogs, and internet chat rooms.

I was definitely persona non grata at the local firing range, if you know what I mean.

Now, I must say that I love our court system, but let's be realistic; it is something of a work in progress. What with judges so out of touch with reality, and with laws so ambiguous that I could drive a truck thru them, it's a wonder that anything ever gets accomplished.

This libel case would be no different. Both sides presented arguments to a judge, who ultimately ignored everyone, and ruled for no one. The court did find merit in the lawsuit but decided further legal action would be required. In his infinite wisdom, the Judge issued a gag order. Because this case still has not been settled, as of this publication, the gag order is still in effect. Hence, my indirect references to a national gun lobbying organization.

Meanwhile, Robyn and I had been living together for quite some time now, yet my emotions were only recently beginning to boil. It started innocently enough; one night, after a lot of drinking, Robyn passed out in my room. I was way too drunk to try and move Robyn to her own bedroom, so I moved her to my bed before I passed out.

The next day, when Robyn woke up in my arms, she didn't protest. Occasionally, Robyn would stay the night in my room. At first, it was one or two nights a week, but lately, it had been every night. It seems that Robyn didn't like to sleep alone. Finally, one night Robyn looked me in the eyes and asked, "Can we be just friends?"

"You tell me," I replied.

"Seriously, can we be just friends?" Robyn repeated.

I responded, "That is something that you have to decide. I just want to be with you; if that means as friends only, then friends it is. However, if you want me to decide, you'll divorce Tom and marry me.

"Why?"

Robyn smiled, "Don't get me wrong I really enjoy this, but…"

"But what about Tom," I finished Robyn's thought.

Robyn nodded, "I do still love him, you know."

"I know," I replied while trying to hide my discomfort.

Robyn continued, "I love you too. It's just that, over the years Tom has been there for me, even before you and I were dating."

"He isn't here now." I was really getting irritated with the way this conversation was going now.

"That's my fault. I wasn't honest with him about us. I know you don't like this, but the biggest difference between you and Tom is that you can remain my friend, even if *this* ends. Tom cannot. I just don't know if I am ready to live my life without Tom."

"Even if that means living it without me?" I was becoming very hostile to the whole idea of Tom.

“You don’t mean that,” Robyn replied. “You might say it, but you don’t really mean it. You’re a better person than that.”

Then Robyn kissed me on the cheek.

“I don’t want this to end! Not now! Not ever! I will not give up on this because you feel guilty!” I raised my voice, the pain I was feeling was very evident to Robyn.

“Hey, I was just being honest with you,” Robyn said as she took my hand and kissed it. “Don’t ever forget that I do love you.”

I looked at Robyn and said, “You have a decision to make, but don’t expect me to make it easy on you.”

“Fair enough,” Robyn replied.

Robyn may have been confused about a lot of things, but God did she know how to drive me wild.

♦♦♦

It was now a couple of weeks later, and Traci ran another special. This one included additional remarks from Alice regarding the latest allegations of Dr. Johnson and Tonya Jones. Also included was an interview with Jane and, appearing for the first time on television ever, Stacey.

Stacey didn't talk, but the interview did show her playing soccer with friends while Jane discussed the decision to hide the truth from me. Jane candidly talked about being forced into her original interview, she also spoke about our shared custody agreement, and offered her opinion of my parenting skills. She said that I had good instincts and would make an excellent father with a little more practice.

The final segment was an interview with Theo Roberts. Traci and Theo discussed his decision to support my defense in the upcoming trial. Theo expressed his desire that I not be convicted of any crime. He further explained that he held no malice towards me and that he had come to terms with his disability.

Theo spoke openly about his physical recovery progress and his psychological epiphany, resulting in a commitment to change his life for the better. Theo apologized for his actions that evening, and he went on to commend me for my actions that night. The whole special was another home run for Traci and my cause.

After the interview aired, Traci called me to see how I was doing. She wanted to know if I could go out for a drink with her and maybe grab a bite to eat. Surprised, I said yes. We met at a little out of the way restaurant near her house. We were seated near the back, out of sight for the most part. During dinner, Traci and I discussed the upcoming trial. Traci seemed genuinely concerned about my spirits, she kept asking about how I was really feeling.

After dinner, she seemed nervous as we were finishing up the last of the wine.

"I have something I need to ask you. You don't have to answer, but I would like to ask you about something of a personal nature."

Surprised, I asked "What is it?"

Shifting around in her seat, Traci glanced back and forth between the wine glass and my eyes. She then asked, "Tell me the truth about you and Robyn. Are you two seeing each other?"

Not sure where Traci was going with this, I responded, "Are you asking as a reporter?"

"No, not as a reporter," Traci answered, "I'm asking as someone who is interested in you."

"No. Robyn is living with me, but we are not dating."

Just as she was about to speak, Traci's phone rang. She looked at the number, and said, "Wait a minute; I've got to take this call."

She answered the phone; as the conversation wore on, I could tell by her facial expressions that she wasn't happy with the caller. When she hung up, she sighed, "David. I'm sorry, but I have to go in to work tonight."

We, I mean she, paid the dinner bill and we headed out to the parking lot. I asked her again, "Why do you want to know if I am dating Robyn?"

"I'll talk to you about it later. Can I call you tonight when I get home?"

I told her to call me whenever she wanted. As Traci was about to leave, she gave me a hug, and kissed me on the cheek. Then she whispered into my ear, "You're so damn cute."

She got in her car and drove away.

After I watched her leave, I headed for my car. As I drove home, I tried to figure out what Traci wanted. Twenty minutes later, and I still had no plausible explanation when I pulled into the driveway. I got out of the car, and as I walked toward the house, Robyn opened the front door.

At first, Robyn was all smiles, and then, without warning, her mood changed…dramatically. Without provocation, I saw a flash of anger in her eyes; seconds later, she slammed the door in my face. Stunned, I opened the door, and Terry was standing inside, just as confused.

I looked at him and asked, “What did I do?”

Terry shrugged, then he said, “You’ve got something on your cheek.” He took a closer look and asked, “Is that lipstick?”

I remember thinking, *Oh Shit!*

I explained to Terry about how Traci kissed me on the cheek. By the time I had finished my explanation, Robyn had already barricaded herself in the bathroom. It took another fifteen minutes of pleading and explaining to get Robyn to open the door.

Later that night, Robyn apologized for her reaction, saying that seeing the lipstick caused an unexpected burst of emotion. Besides, she added, it wasn’t like I was dating Traci or anything. Robyn then went to bed; I on the other hand, waited patiently for Traci’s phone call.

As promised, Traci called. She was still at the station, and she would be there for some time to come. She wanted to know if I could see her the next evening. When I asked where she wanted to meet, she said at her house. She gave me directions and then said goodnight. I finished my drink and then headed to bed.

Already in bed, Robyn awoke as I laid down. She rolled over so that we were face to face. I whispered good night, and then Robyn did something that caught me completely off guard. She ran her hand along my cheek, and in the darkness, she leaned forward and kissed me, passionately.

It was a kiss that I could feel all over if you know what I mean. When Robyn was done kissing me, she said good night and then curled up against me. With the rigidity of my sexual desire pressing firmly against Robyn's inner thigh, she held my hand and then fell asleep again.

When I awoke, Robyn was already gone. I decided that last night's kiss must have been an instinctual reaction to the situation. She must have forgotten where she was, and who she was with, causing her to mistakenly kiss me. With that problem out of the way, I could now focus my attention on Traci's interest in Robyn.

Before I knew it, it was time to leave for Traci's.

Even as I pulled into Traci's driveway, I still did not know why she was asking about Robyn. Throughout the day— I had tried to forget about the mystery, but my mind kept wandering back to the enigma. I kept asking myself, over and over again, why would Traci ask about me dating Robyn?

I had come up with several incredible explanations, but none of them seemed realistic. I walked up the front steps, toward the door, and then rang the bell. From somewhere inside, over the sound of soft jazz music, I heard Traci saying that she would be there in a minute.

Since I had a couple of minutes, I decided to look around and appreciate the front of Traci's house. It was a simple bungalow house on a quiet brick street in the heart of Winter Park. Small by comparison to the behemoths on either side, Traci's house was steeped in character. With a well-manicured lawn and lush landscaping, it looked like a snapshot taken from a *Better Homes & Gardens* magazine cover.

Traci opened the door and invited me in. Dressed in tight fitting jeans and a tank top shirt, Traci looked even better than she did on TV. As I walked in the door, Traci handed me a glass of wine. She led me to the living room, where we sat down and began talking.

She told me about her house, when she bought it, what her plans were for the backyard. We also talked about the upcoming trial and other trivial things. It wasn't until after we opened a second bottle of wine that Traci finally approached the subject of my interest.

Traci said, “I have a confession to make about last night. There was something that I wanted to say to you.”

“I was wondering when you would get to that.” I said.

“Are you really going to make me say it?” Traci asked.

I said, “I wish that you would.”

Traci sighed, “The very first time that I saw you, I thought you were cute. And then, when I saw you fumble your way through your first press conference, I thought you were adorable. And with each passing day, I found myself more and more attracted to you.”

I laughed; looking around, I said, “Is this some kind of joke? Did Terry put you up to this?”

“No. I’m being serious.” Traci replied.

“Why? I mean, I’m just an average guy, and you’re, well you’re you; Traci Kaneko, TV reporter.”

“Aren’t you attracted to me?” She asked.

“Of course, I am,” I replied, “It’s just that, I don’t know…I mean what can I offer you? It can’t be money because I don’t have much, and God knows I’m not the best-looking guy around.”

Traci countered, "To you maybe, but I find you irresistible."

Again, I asked, "Why? I mean, let's be realistic. There are plenty of better men than me. How can I possibly compete?"

Traci continued, "All of the guys that I meet are either trying to impress me with their money or trying to sweep me off my feet with their looks. To them, I'm just a local celebrity with a pretty face, a status symbol. They don't bother to find out who I really am, but not you; you have always treated me as a real person, and not just another pretty face. Truthfully, I find that very attractive."

Still confused, I asked, "But you are so far out of my league."

"David, you are a much greater person than you think."

I shook my head in disbelief, "So, let me get this straight, you want to date me?"

"That's what I'm saying." Traci said as she leaned over and kissed me. "Would you like to see the bedroom?"

When Traci and I were done, my first instinct was to go running down the street screaming at the top of my lungs, *I fucked Traci Kaneko!* But, while still basking in the afterglow of my achievement, I realized that what had just happened was much more powerful than I ever expected.

As we lay there in the darkness, bodies intertwined, we talked about where this would lead. Both of us agreed that it would be a good idea to keep this budding relationship quiet until we were reasonably sure that it would work. In addition, Traci also insisted, and I agreed, that we remain sexually exclusive. Part of the agreement was that I wouldn't stay over until we ever went public, so I got up about two in the morning to go home. A naked Traci walked me to the door and kissed me goodnight.

On the way home, I found myself singing with joy. I hadn't felt this type of connection with anyone since, well, since Robyn.

When I got home, Robyn was already asleep. I tried not to wake her as I climbed into my bed. Being a light sleeper, Robyn woke up anyway. She looked at the clock, made a comment about me being late, and then she kissed me. The whole time I'm thinking, *I'm in some deep fucking shit now*.

Robyn curled up next to me, the arch of her back pressed firmly against my abdomen, and then she fell asleep again.

As expected, the next day Rhonda Spears released another special. Again, this special interviewed Dr. James

Johnson and Tonya Jones. They repeated their claims that I was a ‘racist’, that Alice had forgotten her black heritage, and that the city of Orlando had participated in a huge cover up. For good measure, Rhonda threw in a couple of interviews with local citizens who just so happened to support Dr. Johnson and Tonya Jones.

To me, it was more of the same old shit that we had seen before, just repackaged to look like it was new. Honestly, I had never heard of Rhonda Spears before the incident, but now I wished that I would never hear of her again.

The Offer, The Consequences of Bad Journalism, & The Reveal

A few days later, Alice got a call from the Assistant District Attorney, Sean Walker. It seems that Mr. Walker was ready to make a deal; if I would plead guilty to four counts of involuntary manslaughter, he would recommend that I be sentenced to a couple of years of probation and community service.

Mr. Walker insisted that if I took the deal, I would never serve a single day in jail. Alice responded that she would need to confer with me before any deal could be reached. So, Alice called me on the phone and presented Mr. Walker's proposition. I asked Alice what her thoughts were on the offer. She replied by saying that it wasn't a bad deal.

"Would you take it?" I asked.

"Honestly, no," she responded.

Surprised, I asked, "Why not?"

Alice replied, “David, you didn’t do anything wrong. Walker knows his case is weak, he wouldn’t have offered a deal otherwise. I believe that you will be found innocent during any jury trial.”

“Then fuck it,” I said.

“So, you do not want to take the deal?” Alice asked.

I thought about it for a moment, and meekly replied, “No.”

“Good boy. I’ll talk to you later.” Alice responded.

Shortly after, I learned about the Rhonda Spears debacle when Terry called me to ask if I had seen the news recently. Ever since the *incident*, I had rarely watched television, let alone the news. So, when Terry called, I thought he must have seen something negative about me again. This time it was different; it was Rhonda who was now on the defensive.

It seems that her involvement with the first Jane interview was under attack. Jane’s revelation that she lied about my knowledge of Stacey, at the insistence of Rhonda, was fueling a journalistic backlash. Now it was Rhonda’s turn to feel the uncomfortable pressure of public opinion for a change.

The network released a hastily prepared statement; it stated that the network had no prior knowledge of Rhonda’s "suggestion" that Jane should be less than truthful when it came to my knowledge of Stacey's existence. It went on further to say that any disciplinary action would be taken only after an internal investigation had been completed. I guess it was just a coincidence that Rhonda Spears did not appear on any network, at least for a while.

With everything going on, Terry decided that I needed a little distraction. You know, something to take my mind off of the upcoming trial, Stacey's fast approaching birthday, Robyn, and all the other thoughts swimming around in my head. Terry reasoned that, next to plying me with tequila, golf would be the best activity to help me temporarily forget about the outside world. It was around nine in the morning when Terry called and stated, "Get dressed and grab your clubs."

He gave me twenty minutes to get my act together and clear my busy day of nothing in particular.

A half hour later, we headed out to play golf. It should be noted that I love to play golf. The smell of the great outdoors on a sunny day, the feel of a well-manicured fairway beneath your feet, and the ritualistic male bonding that takes place between mulligans and beers.

Today, Terry decided we were going to play eighteen holes in Zellwood. About thirty minutes outside of Orlando,

Zellwood is world famous for its annual corn festival. Yet, it is also home to an overlooked golf course, one that offers a great deal of elevation changes, for Florida anyway, and some challenging hole-layouts.

To me, a bad day on a golf course is better than any good day at work. Today would be a bad day. I was playing terribly, so bad in fact that by the time we made the turn for the final nine, I was drinking more beers and not making *any* decent shots. It was so bad, that I thought, if only for a second, about giving up the game of golf. When I put my third straight ball into the water on thirteen, I quit playing altogether and concentrated on doing something I was very good at; drinking beer.

It was during the last few holes that I confided to Terry, "I've got a secret."

"What?" Terry asked.

Smirking, I said, "I've been seeing someone."

"Seeing or fucking?" Terry asked as he opened a beer and took a deep drink.

I laughed, "Fucking."

Terry spit the beer out, the spray flying across the golfcart windshield, "No shit! You've been fucking Robyn?"

Trying so hard to contain my excitement, I said, "No, not Robyn!"

Now Terry was dying with curiosity, "Then *who*?"

I said with glee, "Traci."

"Traci who?" Terry asked, once again drinking his beer.

I smiled, "Traci Kaneko."

Once again, Terry spit the beer out, and once again, the spray splashed across the windshield. Terry's response was a resounding, "Bullshit!"

I went on to explain how Traci and I got together. Terry wanted details, but I wasn't about to paint a picture of a naked Traci Kaneko for him; he would have to imagine it like everybody else. After all, I may not be able to keep a secret, but at least I can hold my tongue when it comes to the finer details of lovemaking.

We left the golf course and headed for home, my home. We picked up a case of beer, a pack of cigarettes, and a couple of steaks. The party continued at the house, with Terry asking for more and more details, and me loving every minute of it. We fired up the grill and, in no time, we were dining on an exquisite culinary masterpiece.

Shortly after finishing our feast, Robyn came home. Grabbing a beer, she joined in on our party. The three of us drank, and laughed, and talked under the pale moonlight. Throughout the night, Terry would whisper some smart-ass comment about Traci in my ear, and then look for Robyn's confusion when I laughed. Eventually, Terry passed out in my chaise lounge chair next to the pool. Robyn wanted to move him to the spare bedroom, but I said let Terry sleep outside tonight.

Sometimes, payback is a bitch.

Stacey's Birthday

What do you get for a thirteen-year-old girl? That was my dilemma. I wanted to get her something special, but I didn't want to go overboard either. So finally, I settled on a laptop computer; it was something special yet a practical gift as well.

Ever since we first met, I had been in contact with Stacey on a regular basis. It wasn't every day that we would talk, but we would chat three or four times a week. We also exchanged emails, almost daily. She had finally gotten comfortable with calling me Dad, and I still had not gotten used to that title. It's hard to wake up one day and be a Dad for a pre-teen girl. I missed all the usual milestones and walked straight into the '*Tommy's so cute'* phase of her life. Just around the corner staring me in the face were the dreaded teenage years, her first real crush, and a host of other possibilities that I didn't even want to think about.

Stacey had also started to say I love you; now this was something that, I must admit, scared the hell out of me. It was hard enough just getting through life on your own, now add the pressure of someone else who is relying on you emotionally. With a girlfriend it's easier because you can just walk away any time when things go wrong, but as a father, there is a bond that cannot be shed; no matter how uncomfortable or unworthy that you may feel.

And unworthy I did feel.

I had no idea what I was doing. I was unprepared, and I felt like I was lost in the woods. As a father, I didn't know where I was going, I didn't know how I would get there, and I wasn't sure I could find a solution. But in the back of my mind, or more appropriately, my heart, I felt something that I could not explain. Something that was drawing me into the universe of my child; I just loved how that felt.

On the morning of Stacey's birthday, I called to see how she liked my gift. She was stunned; it was the last thing she expected to get from me. I asked what she did expect to get; she replied maybe a video game, but not in a million years did she expect to get a laptop. Jane thought that I had lost my mind, but I explained to her that I got a good deal on it, and after all, Stacey could use it for school. Stacey ran through the list of everything she got that day; the clothes, soccer stuff, and few other things that I honestly can't remember. It was a good day for me, something I was proud to be part of; I had taken one more baby step on my journey to become a father.

Life, however, finds a way of reminding you where you really stand in the grand scheme of things. It was a few days later when I got a serious reality check, courtesy of a certain Orlando police officer who shall remain nameless. I had been drinking, as usual, and to my dismay I had run out of alcohol. Robyn wasn't home yet, so I decided to make a beer run to the corner store. Once I got there, I decided that I needed something with a little more kick than beer had, so I headed further down the street to the liquor store.

I bought a large bottle of rum, jumped in the car, and headed for home. Between the liquor store and home, there is a traffic light, a traffic light that I, stupidly, ran. If I had been paying more attention, I would have seen the police car that I cut off in the process. I did see the lights in the rearview mirror, however— as the police cruiser pulled in behind me, it just felt like a nightmare about to happen. I could see it now, ADA Walker standing in front of the witness stand regaling the jury about my DUI arrest.

Let the record reflect, I was drunk, I knew it, and as soon as the officer stepped up to my window, she knew it too.

“License, registration, and proof of insurance, please,” she said.

I fumbled around, trying hard not to look drunk, for the registration. Before I could find it, she asked, “Have you been drinking?”

“Just a little,” I confessed.

“Could you please step out of the car,” she responded.

As I stepped out of the car, I handed her my license. She took it and looked at it closely. She looked at me, and then back at the license again. “Are you the guy who shot those thugs downtown a while back?” she asked.

“Yes, I am.” I sheepishly responded.

“Officer Rodriguez is a friend of mine. He’s a good guy, and a good cop,” she hesitated, looked around and then continued, “Where are you going?”

“Home,” I replied.

“How far away is home?” she asked.

I replied, “About a mile up the road.”

“Because you saved the life of a good cop, I’m going to do you a favor. I’m going to take you home. However, if I ever catch you driving again under the influence of alcohol, I *will* throw the book at you. Do you understand me?"

"Yes ma'am." I blurted out. "Thank you so much."

She drove me home, and as she was leaving, she said, "I'm serious. I don't want to ever see you driving again when you've been drinking."

I thanked her again. I decided that it was time for a change; my drinking had become a major problem, and I needed to get it under control. For example, I would frequently pass out on the couch, or out by the pool, only to be roused back to life by Robyn and then promptly told to go to bed. I had memory issues too, I would forget what happened the night before, forget conversations with family or friends. Once, I even broke a glass because I was seeing double and picked the wrong coffee table to set my drink down on. It, of course, shattered into several pieces. The next morning, I thought it was just a dream; until I stepped onto a piece of broken glass.

These were problems, to be sure. Yet, how much of it was me? And how much of it was the circumstance that I found myself in? Before the *incident*, I drank— a lot, but it was never this much. However, I hadn't killed four people, nor been charged with several felonies prior to the *incident* either. Ah, but the taste of rum at sunrise, a glass of whiskey at sunset, or a shot of tequila at midnight would make me smile when nothing else could. It would bring out a warmth inside of me that had been lost so long ago.

What's that line from the Eagles song, *'Some dance to remember, some dance to forget'*? I guess I was dancing to forget, and who wouldn't want to forget that torment? Who wouldn't want to put that— nightmare, in the distant past? In war it's called Post-Traumatic Stress Disorder; for me, it was just the lingering reminder of that Saturday night. A reminder that could be washed away, albeit briefly, inside a bottle of rum, whiskey, gin, vodka, whatever alcohol you had lying around the house. I may have had a drinking problem, but that certainly was eclipsed by my real-world problems.

So, yeah, like that was going to happen.

Dad, it's Me, Stacey

The next day I got a frantic phone call from Stacey.

"Dad, it's me Stacey," she raced between sobs, "Mom's been in a car accident, and she's been hurt real bad."

"What happened?" I nervously asked.

"We were on the way to school when somebody ran a red light and hit us on the driver's side," Stacey cried.

"Are you okay?" I asked in a panic.

The fear in Stacey's voice was palpable.

"I'm fine, but Mom isn't."

"Where is she?" Fearing the worst, I begged.

"She's at the hospital." Stacey sniffled.

Genuinely concerned about Stacey's well-being, I asked, "Where are you?"

Stacey, weak from crying, said, "I'm at the hospital too."

“Listen, everything’s going to be alright,” I said, trying to reassure her, “I’m going to hop on the earliest flight that I can. I’ll be there soon.”

“Please hurry, Dad!” The tone of her voice broke my heart.

“I will,” trying to stay as calm as possible, “Is there anybody who you can stay with until I get there?”

“Yes. Grandpa Jerry.” Stacey sobbed.

It was a relief to know that someone, at least, could be there for her during this scary moment. I said, “Okay. Stay with him, I’ll call you as soon as I get there.”

Somewhere inside, Stacey found the strength to say, “Okay. I love you, Dad.”

“I love you too,” The words came out of my mouth, but the emotion behind them sprung forth from my heart.

The next phone call I made was to Alice. I reached her voicemail; I left a message telling her what was going on. Since my travel had been restricted, Alice would have to notify the proper authorities that I would be in New York for an indefinite amount of time. I checked the flight schedule and booked a seat on the next flight to New York, which was in four hours.

As I was packing the phone rang again, this time it was the New York Police. They informed me that Jane had died from her injuries. I asked if Stacey knew about her Mother's death yet. They stated that she still did not know, so I requested that they wait until her Grandfather had arrived before relaying the terrible news. I hung up the phone, and in a daze, I continued to pack and headed for the airport.

♦♦♦

Within a few days, Jerry, Jane's father, had arranged the funeral. It was an awkward time for me— dealing with Jerry, face to face. When I dated Jane, Jerry did not like me, and apparently after Jane got pregnant— it was even worse. Now here I was trying to make small talk with a man who hated me while preparing for the funeral of his only child.

Stacey was still in shock; she had spoken very little since learning of her Mother's death. When she did talk, her voice was weak and full of apprehension. Stacey was physically and emotionally different; her eyes looked sullen and void of feeling, and her mind drifted in and out of consciousness. Her anxiety, and my lack of knowledge in addressing this type of situation, weighed heavily on my mind. Try as I might, I just couldn't seem to find the words to make everything better; after all, how do you comfort a child who has lost their Mother?

The funeral was held on a dreary, miserable looking Friday; dark clouds hung heavy in the gray sky as the wind howled through the cemetery. After the viewing, a steady line of mourners passed through the cemetery gates moving to the freshly dug grave in the west corner of the lot. As people waited, the pallbearers emerged from the church carrying the casket, and Jane, to their final resting place. As the casket was put in place, the sobs and moans of the grieving merged with the wind to create an eerie chorus of agony.

The Priest said a few brief words and then the service was over. As people milled about chatting about Jane's life and her untimely ending, Stacey stood before the grave. In her hand she held a necklace that I had given Jane many years ago; Stacey rubbed the gold links between her fingers as she looked down into the grave. She looked up to the sky and muttered a small prayer; once more Stacey looked down into the grave and then crossed herself. As she unclasped the necklace and put it around her neck, a tear gently rolled down her cheek.

Later that day, Jerry and I were sitting in the kitchen of his house; neither one of us had said a word to one another since leaving the funeral. All day, people would be coming by to convey their condolences, and it was when Stacey left the kitchen to answer the door that Jerry finally spoke up.

"What will become of Stacey?" his voice quivered as he waited for my verdict.

Legally, I had the right to assume custody of Stacey. Morally, however, I was standing on rapidly shifting sand. After a brief moment of contemplation, I answered, "I don't know. I thought that since there are only a couple more months of school left that she could stay here with you until summer break."

"And then what?" Jerry grimaced in anticipation of my response.

"Then I thought she could come stay with me for the summer," I responded.

"And after that?" Jerry persisted.

I hadn't thought about after that. I hadn't thought about how Jerry might feel about that. I took a minute, collected my thoughts, and said, "I think that Stacey is old enough to make her own decision about where she wants to be."

"And if she decides she wants to come back here?" Jerry asked.

I hadn't thought about that either. God, I'm terrible at this Father stuff. Unsure of the outcome, I responded, "Then I would respect her decision. Jerry, I know we have had our differences in the past, but this isn't about us now. It's about Stacey and what's best for her. I'm not here to steal your granddaughter away from you."

Jerry's curiosity had finally gotten the best of him, "Then why are you here?"

"Because my daughter needs me." The words coming out of my mouth even surprised me, but that I actually meant them, terrified me for some reason.

Jerry asked me then, genuinely confused.

"Why aren't you being the asshole that I remember?"

Finally! After all these years, I felt his hatred of me begin to crumble, even if only a little bit. I answered with the most adult thing that I had ever said in my life—

"Because I'm not a teenage boy anymore...I'm a father now."

It was during this stressful time, that Traci and I took a major step in our relationship. When Traci first heard about Jane's death, she wanted to come with me to New York. Stupidly, I decided that her presence would be an issue for Stacey and Jerry, so I told her to stay in Orlando. Immediately, I regretted my decision, but I could not bring myself to rescind the words.

Every day, during my stay in New York, Traci and I would talk on the phone. It was during one of these conversations, that I made an admission. We were talking about my feelings and the funeral, when I let loose the three most powerful words in the English language, "I love you."

To my surprise, Traci responded in kind, "I love you too."

Ever since that day, every one of our conversations began, and ended, with the same three words. To my surprise, I honestly meant it; I really loved Traci.

Now the question was what to do about Robyn?

I needed to address my lingering feelings for Robyn, and yet, I didn't want to admit my weakness. I had always hoped that Robyn would leave Tom, but I had never considered the possibility that I would be in love with somebody else. So now here I was, for the first time since I had met Robyn, faced with the real possibility of life without her. I was torn; Traci was a dream come true, but Robyn was a wish unfulfilled.

Time was no longer on my side; I had to make a decision. As good as Traci was, she would have to cede my love to Robyn, provided Robyn would have me. I knew, deep inside, that I could not pursue my relationship with Traci without first offering my soul to Robyn.

The Long Way Home

I had to return to Orlando the next day. As fate would have it, my flight was delayed for three hours due to weather conditions at the airport. My flight was scheduled to leave at 9:15 PM, and I wouldn't be leaving until sometime after midnight, putting me in Orlando approximately at 3 in the morning. Robyn had agreed to pick me up before the delay, so I called her and told her I would take an Uber home instead.

Since there wasn't a lot I could do, I started thinking about my life, and how screwed up it was. There were many things that I could not change, but there was one area of my life that I could possibly focus on, my relationship with Robyn, or Traci. Since I didn't know exactly what to say to Robyn about Traci, I thought that it would be best to write my thoughts out on a piece of paper; that way, I could edit my thoughts without spewing out a load of nonsense. I sat down at the bar, ordered a beer, and started writing.

The following is what came out of my head and made it on to paper:

Dear Robyn:

Recent events have led me to reevaluate certain aspects of my life. I used to believe that I was invincible, that I would live forever, but now a stark reality has come to the surface of my thoughts. It seems odd to me that the death of four strangers did not touch me like the death of Jane. Her passing has me questioning my own mortality, and the very value of my existence.

There are many things that I regret, and yet, there are only so many things that I can change. Time is running out on my life, and still fate has left me with so many unanswered questions concerning our relationship.

Do you miss doing the things that we used to do? When you are in the throes of passion, do you think of me? Do you find yourself picturing a life together? Are you comfortable with the reality that one of us might die before we make love again?

I know that I have said, many times in the past, that I am comfortable with us being just friends; however, I find myself wanting more.

I tell you this now; because there has been a development that you should know about. Over the last few weeks, I have discovered feelings for another woman, feelings that I thought not possible without you. However, before I can possibly explore these feelings any further, I need to know what you want. I know the answers that I seek are unfair to ask of you, but no one ever said that life was fair. Life is but a flicker of light in the dark, a mystery that ends all too soon.

How this ride should end, I leave to you.

Love always,

David

♦♦♦

It was nearly 4 AM when I finally made it home. Robyn, wearing one of my T-shirts, was sound asleep in my bed. As I entered the room, she mumbled something about being glad I made it home okay and then rolled over and went back to sleep. I showered, brushed my teeth, and headed for my first decent sleep in many days. Before climbing in to bed I placed my note in Robyn's purse. Once I was under the sheets, Robyn rolled back over and put her arm around me. I fell asleep a few minutes later with Robyn's head on my shoulder.

The next morning Robyn was up early; to be sure not to disturb me, she got ready in the spare bathroom. Robyn had a cup of coffee and headed out the door. It wasn't until after Robyn got to work that she found my note. She read it, and then read it again. Robyn then got up from her desk and locked her office door. She sat back down in her chair and tears rolled down her cheeks as she began to sob uncontrollably.

She cried for what felt like hours before anyone realized there might be a problem. Terrified that her emotional breakdown would become the talk of the office, Robyn decided to leave. She left a voicemail message telling her manager that she was leaving for the day due to a family emergency. Before anyone could question her about the emergency, she snuck out the side door and headed for home.

Robyn ignored the repeated phone calls on her cell phone while she struggled to hold it together long enough for her to make it home. When she looked up, she was at her house, Tom's house, not at mine. Robyn put the car in park and cried some more. When she felt that she had cried herself out and could now drive again, she headed to my house. Once there she entered my bedroom, where I was still sleeping, and threw the note at me.

"What's this?" Robyn shouted.

Stunned, I shook my head and tried to focus my eyes on the note.

"It's a note." I dryly replied.

Not amused by my attempt at humor, Robyn shouted at me again, "Why are you doing this?"

"Doing what?" I asked as I climbed out of bed.

"Hurting me," Robyn was in tears again.

"I'm not trying to hurt you," I said as I tried to comfort her. "I'm trying to tell you how I feel."

Robyn pulled away from me and continued, "Well, you are hurting me!"

Dumfounded I asked, "How?"

"You know that I love you. You also know that I am married to Tom. You know what you are asking of me isn't fair." Robyn squeaked out between sobs.

I asked, "And it's okay for you to sleep with me, in my bed, and I'm not supposed to want more. How is that fair to me?"

"It's not," she replied, "But you don't understand."

"Understand what?" I insisted.

"How does this make me feel? I feel guilty for wanting a physical relationship with you because of Tom, and yet, I feel guilty for not having a physical relationship with you because I love you. I can't win, and it's driving me fucking crazy."

"*Then make a fucking decision!*" I shouted.

"Who is she?" Robyn demanded.

"Traci." Well, that was easier to say than I thought it would be.

Incredulous, Robyn demanded, "What? How?"

"It just sort of happened," I said, "I'll leave her if you want me to, but you have to choose. Tom or me."

"I can't. I can't let go of either of you." Robyn confessed.

"What am I supposed to do? Sit here and fucking wait for you to make up your mind? I can't do that anymore.

"*Life's too fucking short for that!*" I barked.

By now, Robyn was on the bed in a fetal position crying. I sat back down next to her and put my hands on her, this time she didn't pull away. I hung my head in shame and whispered, "I'm sorry. I didn't mean to hurt you. It's just that I love you so much and I want more than you can give me at this time."

I kissed her cheek and wrapped my arms around her. The two of us lay there entwined for a while before we both fell asleep from emotional exhaustion. It was early evening before we awoke.

Although Robyn was no longer crying, things were different that night. We barely said a word to each other as we ate dinner. After dinner, Robyn said that she was not feeling well and went to bed. I, on the other hand, could not sleep at all; there was so much swirling around in my mind. I wanted so badly discuss this with someone, anyone; but who could I turn to?

First, I tried to call Traci, but she was busy at work. Then I tried Terry, but he wasn't home either. I actually considered calling Stacey, but it was way past her bedtime. I definitely did not want to talk to Mom and Dad about my situation.

Question— So what does an average guy, with women troubles, do when he is not able to talk to a real person?

Answer— He starts drinking and hopes to God that something decent is on TV.

I flipped through the channels, looking for something to watch. Just before giving up in frustration, I came across one of my favorite movies, *Casablanca*. It had just started, and I was all set to get lost in the movie. Instead, the movie motivated me; if Bogart can do the right thing, then so could I. It would be painful, but it was the right thing to do, for the women that I loved.

The next morning, I decided to call Tom. I waited until after Robyn left for work again before I picked up the phone. After a couple of rings, Tom answered the phone.

"Hello?"

"Hello Tom, it's me David."

"What do you want? Robyn's not here!" Tom raged.

"Tom, you're being an asshole. Robyn thinks the world of you," I stated.

"I don't give a fuck what Robyn thinks!" Tom angrily replied.

I responded, "Yes, you do. If you didn't, then you would have kicked my ass years ago."

"What do you want?" Tom repeated.

"To tell you that you are making a big mistake," I replied.

"Fuck you! I know that Robyn's been living with you! Do you think I'm stupid? I know what you two have been doing!" Tom lashed out at me.

"Tom, we haven't done anything, yet. If you don't fix this soon you will lose her forever," I responded. "Yeah, she loves me, but she loves you just a little bit more."

"Why are you telling me this?" Tom asked.

"It's not for you, it's for Robyn." I conceded, "Her happiness is more important than my own happiness, or yours."

After a long pause, Tom's confusion was evident, "Thanks, I guess."

I continued, "Remember, as far as Robyn is concerned, this conversation never took place."

Still confused, Tom said, "Okay."

"Oh, and Tom, this will be the only warning you will ever get from me. If you don't act now, I will steal her away from you.

"The choice is yours to make," I said just before I hung up the phone.

Meanwhile, on the other side of town…

Shortly after I made my phone call, Robyn was also on the phone. She called Traci from work, Traci answered, “This is Traci Kaneko. Can I help you?”

“Traci, this is Robyn. We need to talk.”

Looking at her clock, Traci said, “Now is not a good time. Can I call you later?”

“No”, Robyn said, “We need to talk now about David.”

Hesitantly, Traci replied, “Oh. So, you know.”

With a flash of anger in her voice, Robyn declared, “Yes, I do!”

“No matter what you say, it will not change my feelings about David.”

“So, you do love him?” Robyn asked.

Traci confirmed, “Yes…yes, I do.”

Robyn hesitated; her heart was aching as she said, “Good for you.”

Surprised, Traci asked, “What?”

A cold shiver went up Robyn’s spine as she said, “David’s happiness is more important than my own, or yours.”

“What are you trying to say, Robyn?”

In a moment of clarity, Robyn finally admitted the truth, out loud for herself, and for Traci to hear.

"That David deserves the best that you can offer."

Suspicious, Traci replied, "I didn't expect this from you."

That flash of anger was back again, Robyn bristled, "It's not for you, it's for David."

"Robyn, thank you for your honesty," Traci said.

Trying very hard to control the anger, the jealously bubbling up inside, Robyn addressed, "Traci, understand this; if you hurt David, I will kick your fucking ass."

"Is that a threat?" A defensive Traci countered.

"No. It's a fact." A dejected Robyn declared.

Traci's anger was now starting to build as she said, "Don't threaten me."

"This is not a threat. This is merely a discussion between two women who love the same man," Robyn concluded the conversation.

Opening Day – The Latest Trial of the Century

Weeks of preparation would soon be put to use as my trial date quickly approached. It's odd how something so distant seems to sneak up on you and then overwhelm your senses. It was only the night before the trial was set to begin that I finally realized my life, my future, depended on what twelve strangers believed my intent was on that fateful evening. I would be a free man, or I would spend the next twenty years of my life in jail.

The possible outcome seemed more frightening than the actual shooting.

I couldn't sleep that night, my mind spun wildly out of control as I tried to picture the trial. Minutes turned into hours, and before I knew it, Alice and I were on my way to the courthouse. Waiting for me was an army of reporters asking every conceivable question as I struggled up the steps of the courthouse. Without acknowledging the rowdy crowd, I quickly made my way through security and to the inner sanctum of the grand building.

As we walked, Alice reiterated our strategy and assured me that justice would prevail. As we waited impatiently for the courtroom to open, I looked around nervously for my security blanket: Robyn. She was there sitting with Terry, waiting to offer me support. Since they both were set to testify, neither could be in the courtroom during the trial.

Mr. Walker stood up from his desk and addressed the court.

"Thank you, your honor.

"Ladies and gentlemen of the jury, we are gathered here today, in this court of law, to decide the fate of an admitted killer. Yes, this man, David Alan Taylor, has admitted to picking up a gun and firing it with the intent to kill. Unfortunately, he successfully killed four out of the five young men he intended to harm. The fifth, Theo Roberts, is confined to a wheelchair for the rest of his life.

"The defense will try to confuse you, most likely using physiological terms, and words like '*intent*', '*self-defense'*, and '*political pressure'* trying to justify the actions of the defendant. But your obligation is to judge based solely on the facts of the case, not the desperate tactics of the defense.

"The facts of the case are very simple; the defendant killed four young men in the prime of their lives, paralyzed another, and he needs to be held accountable for his actions. I know that the task in front of you is a daunting one, but it is your responsibility, as citizens of this great state, to find the defendant guilty."

It was Alice's turn in the spotlight; she rose from her desk and began to speak.

"Ladies and gentlemen of the jury, you have been chosen for this case because you have exhibited the traits characteristic of all good jurists: honesty, integrity, and an open mind. These traits will serve you well in deciding the fate of Mr. David Alan Taylor in this, the most important trial of his young life.

"The prosecution and I do agree on one thing: Mr. Taylor *did* fire the gun, however, the one thing you cannot afford to do as a jurist is make a presumption of guilt without first understanding the extenuating circumstances behind this tragedy. To make such a presumption prior to these proceedings would be a grave injustice, not only for Mr. Taylor, but also the entire legal system.

"How and why Mr. Taylor made the choice to fire the gun is the real story. Our case will show how the gun came to be in Mr. Taylor's hands that night, and what events led up to the shooting. You will learn of the violent crimes committed by the supposed victims earlier in the evening.

"You will hear how Calvin Jones stalked and then subsequently shot Officer Paul Rodriguez in the back. You will be shown the weapons these alleged thugs were armed with, and the devastating wounds suffered by Mr. Taylor.

"Let's face it; this trial is only about racial tensions. There is no other logical reason for this trial. There certainly isn't any evidence to support the Prosecution's case. Once all the evidence has been presented, I know that you will find David Alan Taylor not guilty of the politically motivated crimes he has been charged with by the State."

What follows is an abbreviated record of the trial. The actual trial's transcript numbers more than 700 pages which are, for the most part, boring. I have included what I consider to be the most interesting parts of the trial. For a full transcript, please contact my lawyer.

The prosecution introduced photographic evidence from the security systems downtown that showed the shooting. The prosecution also presented testimony from several witnesses on the scene who stated that I never warned Calvin Jones before shooting him in the head. Under cross-examination most admitted that they believed Calvin would have killed Officer Rodriguez.

Mr. Walker also presented testimony from the medical examiner, Detective Chris Welles, and other officials who detailed the wounds inflicted on the dead and wounded, produced a timeline, and a diagram showing the locations and shots fired by all involved in the shootout. Under a determined cross-examination, Detective Welles and the others admitted that they could not rule out the possibility that Calvin would have killed Officer Rodriguez. In addition, Detective Welles reluctantly admitted using the word *'nigger'* and receiving "pressure" from superiors to secure a confession from me.

Theo Roberts, who was also called to testify, was limited to Yes and No answers by Mr. Walker regarding the events of that evening. There was no mention of the robbery or assault, that is, until Alice's cross-examination. Only after many strenuous objections from Mr. Walker did Theo get the opportunity to express his true feelings.

Theo said that he regretted his role in the assault and robbery, and that he did not hold me responsible for what happened to him, or the others. Theo also stated that the prosecution had offered him immunity for the robbery and assault charges, in exchange for favorable testimony, a deal which Theo initially turned down. When asked why he turned down the prosecution's offer, Theo replied that the experience had changed him as a person; he felt that he needed to be held accountable for his actions, by God and by the law.

Terry, Chris, and Lynn were all called to testify by Mr. Walker. Their testimony was essentially the same: we went out, had a few drinks, and were on our way to another club when the shooting started. Mr. Walker was able to wrest Robyn's secrecy about our relationship from my friends, but Mr. Walker could not get anyone to admit any details about the shooting that had not been introduced in previous testimony.

In a move that was expected by Alice, Robyn was also called to testify by Mr. Walker. Once on the stand, Mr. Walker attacked Robyn's relationship with me. First, Mr. Walker berated Robyn for lying to Tom— he inferred that our relationship was sexual in nature, and attempted to portray Robyn as manipulative woman, intent on getting her way at any cost.

Throughout the whole ordeal, Alice objected after nearly every single question. The judge threatened Mr. Walker with contempt if he did not alter his line of questioning. Robyn cried, but she never broke under the pressure applied by the prosecution.

For me, sitting quietly and listening was an agonizing process as Robyn's character was assailed over and over again. It required all my strength to do nothing while this spectacle unfolded before my very eyes. It wasn't until later that I learned Mr. Walker had verbally attacked Robyn in order to induce an angry reaction from me.

His hope was that I would lose my temper and then try to assault him in the courtroom, thus portraying me as an angry man looking for a fight. However, he would later apologize to Robyn, saying that it was just a legal strategy, and not a personal attack.

Mr. Walker's accusation, unintentionally, also prompted a revelation. As you know, Traci and I had been secretly seeing each other; and, especially now with the trial, we struggled to separate our private and public lives. Since the beginning of the trial, Traci had to just sit there and pretend that what was happening to me did not hurt her, and I couldn't publicly look to her for support. It was agony for both of us. Somehow, somewhere, something had to give. It was becoming apparent that our relationship had reached a critical stage— public acknowledgement.

That night, Traci and I had a serious discussion about the consequences of going public with our relationship. After weighing both the pros and the cons of a public admission, we jointly decided that the time had come to share our news. She placed a late-night call to, and left a message for, the General Manager at the station. Traci wanted her to know about our relationship, prior to any announcement. I too, had to make a few phone calls. I had to officially tell my parents, Terry, and Alice. As an added bonus, I was able to finally stay overnight.

Our normal trial routine was an early morning phone call; a call that could last anywhere from five minutes, right up until the very second that I opened the car door at the courthouse. We would arrive separately, and once inside the courtroom, I would locate Traci in the crowd. When I would see her, I would touch the left side of my face with my left hand. Traci would then touch the right side of her face with her right hand. It was our own little secret way of saying, *I love you.* To our surprise, no one had picked up on our gestures.

Ever since the beginning of the trial, everyone had assumed that Traci had been a diligent journalist. After our upcoming entrance, however, she would be right in the thick of it with me, just the way she wanted it to be.

The next morning, Traci and I made a couple of changes to our routine. First, we started the day with sex, ate breakfast, and then followed that with more sex. Then, we showered together, dressed, and then headed to the courthouse together. When we arrived at the courthouse and the limo door opened, we stepped out into the glare of the media spotlight. Traci held my hand, as we worked our way through the maze of people. Once we reached the front door, Traci gave me a small kiss, just to make sure everyone knew.

Our little display was definitely the talk of the town that night. It seems that an average guy on trial, facing the repercussions of racial tensions, won't get the city talking to one another. However, when an average guy is on trial, facing the repercussions of racial tensions, and is dating a great looking local celebrity, it gets everyone talking.

Tell me, does America have its priorities screwed up, or what?

Once the prosecution was done, it was our turn to present evidence.

Alice called a handful of witnesses, including a police tactics expert. The police tactics expert was a retired New York Police Officer who was a member of the S.W.A.T. team. He testified that Officer Rodriguez had followed proper police procedure by not directly engaging the robbery suspects before back-up could arrive.

I did not testify; I wanted to, but Alice made a tactical decision to deny Mr. Walker a chance to cross-examine me on the stand. Alice had kept our case short, simple, and to the point, resting after less than one day's worth of testimony. After Alice rested our case, it was the prosecution's turn for closing arguments. Mr. Walker stood up and addressed the jury.

"Ladies and gentlemen of the jury, during this trial you have heard testimony from a variety of people, from all walks of life. And although they may have very different opinions about why and how this terrible crime took place, they all agree on the basic facts of this case. I remind you, that as a member of any jury, you are to judge based solely on the facts of a case.

"The basic facts of this case are this: the defendant *shot* and *killed* four young men and wounded two others; this is not in question. It is your responsibility to hold the defendant accountable for his actions and to let the country know that vigilantism will not be tolerated in this state.

"Thank you."

Now it was Alice's turn.

"Ladies and gentlemen of the jury, the prosecution has asked you to forget all the laws of reality in order to convict Mr. Taylor. Yes, Mr. Taylor did fire a weapon that night, however it wasn't *his* weapon. The gun belonged to Officer Rodriguez, who had just been shot in the back by Calvin Jones.

"Calvin Jones and the other alleged thugs brought stolen, or otherwise illicitly gained guns, to downtown that night; they robbed and nearly beat another man to death, and they almost killed Mr. Taylor as well. To convict Mr. Taylor of this act of heroism would be the most tragic miscarriage of justice that this state has ever witnessed.

"Mr. Taylor and I would like to thank you for your time and consideration in this matter."

Suddenly, my fate rested with the jury. It was a curious sensation to put my life in the hands of these complete strangers. I have never been a religious person, however, I found myself praying to God as the jury left for deliberation. I had found the strength to act that dangerous night, but now, here in the safety of a courtroom, I could not move; paralyzed by my fear of the verdict.

Would they understand my motivation, could they sympathize with my dilemma? Would they find me innocent, or would they send me to jail?

The answers to these questions depended on the jury's interpretation of the evidence. Still, it was anyone's guess how long it would take for a decision to be reached. I had wanted to be vindicated; I had wanted my actions to be justified. I had wanted a lot of things, but here I was, stuck in this agonizing purgatory.

As my future hung in the balance, each passing minute felt like a lifetime in solitude. I could feel the weight of the world pressing down on me, slowly crushing the life out of me, as I hopelessly struggled to remain in control of my emotions. Fortunately, I would not have to wait long to hear my fate.

Within hours of beginning deliberation, the jury had reached a verdict. Word of the speedy decision spread quickly throughout the courthouse, and beyond, as the World waited anxiously for a legal answer to the question of my guilt. Proponents on either side of the moral debate felt that it was a good sign for their cause that the jury had fulfilled its obligation in a relatively short timeframe. Without knowing the outcome, I was actually glad it was over.

My life had been, more or less, on hold since that night, and now I could move on and begin the next phase. Guilty or innocent, it didn't really matter to me anymore; for tomorrow morning the World would finally have an answer to a question that had been plaguing me since the start of this ordeal.

We gathered in the courtroom, both friends and adversaries, waiting for the jury to return. The jury entered the packed room and I stood in anticipation of the verdict.

"Has the jury reached a verdict?" The judge asked the jury foreman.

"Yes, your honor. We have," The jury foreman responded.

The foreman passed a piece of paper to a bailiff, who in turn handed it to the judge. The judge opened the paper and then asked the jury to render its verdict. The foreman looked down at his notes and began to read:

"We the jury, find the defendant, David Alan Taylor, *not guilty* of the charge of second degree murder…"

The crowd erupted, some cheering, some crying out in disgust. Mr. Walker slammed his pen on the desk as Alice hugged me and then I jumped up and down in a moment of unrestrained joy. Shouts of *Murderer!* and *Thank God!* simultaneously filled the courtroom. The judge demanded order in the court, and eventually, as a hush fell over the room, the jury foreman continued:

"We the jury, find the defendant, David Alan Taylor, *not guilty* of the charge of attempted murder…" Again, the crowd went wild, and again the judge sought to restore order to his courtroom. After several tense minutes, the room returned to silence. The jury foreman continued, "We the jury, find the defendant, David Alan Taylor, *guilty* of discharging a firearm within city limits."

"David Alan Taylor, I sentence you to one-year probation and fine you five-hundred dollars for discharging a firearm within city limits.

"Court dismissed…" the judge responded.

The courtroom went wild again as the judge imposed his sentence. The pandemonium was too much for the judge and he ordered for the courtroom to be cleared. The bailiffs moved every one of the spectators out of the courtroom, into the hall, and on to the front steps. Inside, as I thanked Alice for the terrific job that she had done, tears streamed down my face.

As we left the courthouse, Alice, Traci, and I were met by an eager media mob waiting to record a juicy sound bite. Reporters were shouting out questions, one on top of another, creating a terrible noise. Bright video lights blinded our eyes as microphones were shoved into our faces.

Through all the confusion, one question caught my attention— "Do you feel vindicated as a hero?"

I stopped, and before I could help myself; I found the following cheesy words— "I am not a hero, I did what I thought was right. If you want a hero, look to the police officers that stand between us and the criminals, look to the firefighters that risk their lives to pull us from burning buildings, look to the soldiers that protect this great nation.

"Look just about anywhere but me, I am not a hero. I am just a guy that would like to be left alone and spend time with my family.

"Thank you and goodbye."

As we were whisked away from the media mob, I crawled into the car and thanked Alice for everything she had done for me. She replied that it was her honor to help such a fine young man find justice in an unjust world. She went on to ask, what's next? I said that it was a new day for me; that I could finally get back to my life with Traci and my daughter. Alice knew that this was not over, but she didn't want to ruin my moment, so she decided to keep her mouth shut and wait until later before she told me what would happen next.

The next day Alice called to tell me the news. Tonya Jones had filed a complaint in civil court against me, claiming that I violated the civil rights of her boys, Calvin and Curtis. Mrs. Jones was suing me for an amount of eight-million dollars per son. I asked Alice can she do that, and Alice replied that yes, she can.

I remember asking what we can do now, and I distinctly remember Alice saying that, as a civil case, the odds of a successful defense were greatly reduced. The burden of proof was less demanding than in a criminal case and the fact that the Jones' were black, and that I was white did not bode well for me in the civil case. I told Alice that I had no money to settle with and I felt that I had nothing to lose. Alice responded by saying that it didn't matter anyway, Mrs. Jones appeared to be in it for the publicity and that she did not see Mrs. Jones trying to settle this lawsuit out of court.

Stacey Comes to Town

The school year had finally finished, and Stacey headed south for the summer.

It was wonderful to see her again— nearly three months after the last time that I saw her in New York. We tried to go about our lives as normal as possible, but the upcoming civil trial and publicity kept getting in the way. Whenever we would try to leave the house, it seemed as if some news agency or another was waiting outside to try and get a sound bite for the evening news. There was a lot of fighting going on as well.

Ever since Jane's death, Stacey had been withdrawn and distant. I had tried, on several occasions, to talk to Stacey about it, but she refused to discuss the topic. When talking didn't work, I turned to pleading. When pleading didn't work, I turned to nagging. Eventually, nagging gave way to frustration, and frustration led to yelling. The two of us bickered about everything; the clothes she wore, the hours she kept, and a million other inconsequential details of a young girl's life.

On numerous occasions, I asked Stacey if she just wanted to go live with Grandpa Jerry. She would always say no, but I could tell that she was having doubts about living with me. And then there was the matter of Traci.

Since Traci and I went public about our relationship, we had spent a lot of time together. Sometimes, by my own admission, too much time together. The three of us would go places together, like a true family, even when I knew Stacey just wanted it to be the two of us. Although Stacey had never seen Jane and me together, it was hard on a girl, to watch her dad in love with anyone but her mother. Stacey didn't understand, just months after the death of her Mom, how I could possibly be in love with someone else.

The summer was ending, and soon Stacey would have to decide about where she wanted to be, New York or Orlando. We would talk about it from time to time, but Stacey remained uncommitted when it came to declaring a destination. Finally, one night, just a few days before the last possible date to decide, Stacey came to my room.

She said, "Dad, I think I want to stay here with you."

Trying to hold back my joy, I asked, "Oh? Are you sure?"

She replied, "Yeah, I'm sure. I just can't go back to New York right now. It reminds me of how much I miss Mom."

"What about your friends?" I asked.

"I'll make new ones," she responded.

The next day would prove to be interesting. Rhonda Spears had been suspiciously silent ever since her dismissal from network news. She would, however, make a comeback. When I heard about Rhonda, she was doing an interview with Carl Tucker. During this interview, Rhonda made some spectacular claims; claims that could change the entire perception of my legal woes.

She claimed that she was instructed to *"trash"* my reputation and offered proof of her accusation. In her hands, Rhonda held a file that she claimed was provided to her, by the assistant to the president of the most powerful national gun lobbying organization in the country.

The file contained confidential information regarding my personal life. Also, in the file, were handwritten notes suggesting areas of vulnerability and concern. One page showed Jane's name circled in bright red ink, and a note in the margin that clearly stated:

USE THIS!

♦♦♦

Within days, Rhonda was making the talk show circuit. Rhonda offered further proof to substantiate her claims during her fifteen additional minutes of fame. She released excerpts from email communications and voice mail records that clearly showed a concerted effort to discredit me. In addition, Rhonda named a senior news executive as a liaison between her and the English couple who provided one of the two known videotapes of the entire incident.

At some point during her tour, Rhonda let it be known that she would soon be hosting a talk show on another national network. I found it very convenient that her public admission would coincide with a disclosure of this magnitude.

Not surprisingly, I was offered the initial segment on the very first episode of Rhonda's show. I declined the opportunity, not because of my fear of cameras, but because of my issues with Rhonda's coverage of the *incident*. However, as luck would have it, someone else *was* available, Alice Miller.

Things started out relatively normal, with Rhonda and Alice exchanging pleasantries to begin the show. For the first couple of minutes, they stuck to small talk, but things took a quick turn when Rhonda asked, "What role, do you think systemic racism played in the shooting deaths of Calvin Jones, Curtis Jones, William Baker, and Marcus Porter?"

I could see it in Alice's eyes, Rhonda had just, unwittingly, lit the fuse, now it was only a matter of time. "Systemic racism was once an issue in this country," Alice began, "Laws were put into place to ensure that black people could not take their proper place in society, then the Civil Rights Act of 1964 was signed into law by President Lyndon B. Johnson on a Thursday—"

Rhonda interrupted, "Can we please get back to the question?"

"You asked a question and I intend to answer it," Alice retorted, "When my parents first met, they weren't allowed to go into a restaurant in their own neighborhood because of the color of their skin. Some years later, they were able to buy that same restaurant. That restaurant paid for me to go to college, and then law school—"

"I'm not sure how this is relevant—" Rhonda quipped.

Alice demanded, "Don't interrupt me! I would not be here today if systemic racism were still a problem! Individual racism, however, is alive and well in America, and, unfortunately, it is not just limited to white people. Black people are just as guilty for judging people by the color of their skin.

Judging each other by how dark, or light, their own skin might happen to be—"

"But what about—"

"I am a black woman who is at the top of my profession," Alice continued, despite Rhonda's attempt to redirect, "Respected by my peers, not because of the color of my skin, but because of my commitment and skill when it comes to seeking justice for my clients. In fact, some of the most respected people in America today are black. Actors, athletes, businessmen and businesswomen, politicians, musicians, we have become an integral part of America..."

Still trying to regain control, Rhonda asked, "I still don't—"

Alice shut Rhonda down again, "The only thing holding us back from reaching our true potential is our own prejudices, and a victim mentality. We are better than this, and yet we abdicate our responsibility to our children, we blame white people for our own failings; we do not take responsibility for our own actions. Being black has nothing to do with being poor and uneducated, but it has everything to do with how we approach life and move the next generation forward."

Again, not sure if I have ever said it aloud before, but God I love Alice Miller.

Another Court Date

After Mrs. Jones filed the civil suit, the presiding judge set a court date. This trial would be very different; the Attorney would be allowed to make race the main issue. This upcoming trial actually scared me more than the criminal trial. In a criminal trial, the prosecution has to show guilt beyond a reasonable doubt.

In a civil trial, all they had to do is convince the jury that there is a reasonable doubt of innocence. Although my freedom was no longer in jeopardy, I now faced the very real prospect of financial ruin. At least in prison they feed you three times a day, without any money who knows when your next meal will come.

Once again, I found myself on the steps of a courthouse, surrounded by the media, and in fear of my future. At least this time Stacey would be by my side throughout the upcoming trial. We passed through the media gauntlet without pausing to comment and headed for the courtroom. Once inside, Alice and I went over our strategy one last time. Our defense would be based on self-defense; the race of the dead was never an issue in my mind. Theo Roberts had refused to participate in the civil suit, yet he would still reluctantly have to testify. All too soon, the court was called to order and the trial was set to begin.

Mrs. Jones' Attorney did not waste any time attacking me as a racist. They inferred my lack of black friends was by choice, not by chance. The attorney referenced the ratio of black workers and white workers hired by me as proof of a racial prejudice on my part. The fact that only a handful of black applicants had ever applied did not seem to matter. I was being run over, and the judge was allowing it; almost every single one of Alice's objections was overruled.

Now it was Alice's turn to present our case. It was, more or less, the same defense as the criminal trial, with a few twists. Alice called a bunch of people from my past and present to testify. Now this was a calculated risk, considering my checkered past.

She asked them if they had ever heard me use the word *'nigger'* or say anything disparaging about blacks in general. Each one testified that they had never heard me say such a thing. Alice concluded her defense by stating that she had spent a great deal of time with me, and as a black woman, she had never felt or perceived any racial prejudice from me.

Once again, my fate rested with a panel of strangers, and once again, the anxiety of an unknown future twisted my emotions into knots. Would the jury believe the facts, as presented by Alice, or would the jury buy in to the outrageous notion that I acted out of racial prejudice?

This time, however, the jury would take much longer to decide, three days to be exact. And as the minutes rolled into hours, and hours to days, emotionally my body quivered in fear. By the time word touched us that the jury had reached a verdict, I was a shell of my former self. So wracked with doubt and fear, I resembled a startled deer caught in the headlights of impending doom.

As the jury filed back into the courtroom, I tried, without success, to read the expressions on their faces. Not one person gave me any indication of the looming verdict. After the jury was seated and the court called to order, the judge asked, "Has the jury reached a verdict?"

The stony voice of the jury foreman replied, "Yes, your honor. We have."

Pausing for a moment to unfold a piece of paper, the foreman then continued.

"We the jury, find the defendant guilty of violating the civil rights of Curtis and Calvin Jones. We also find the defendant responsible for the untimely deaths of Curtis and Calvin Jones."

The judge beat his gavel as cheers rose throughout the courtroom, and said, "Order! Order in the court!"

Once the din had died down the judge went on to ask, "Has the jury reached a decision regarding financial restitution?"

The foreman replied, "Yes, your honor. We have. We find for the plaintiff in the amount of six million dollars."

Against a chorus of boos, hisses, and cries of disgust, the judge sought to regain order in his court. After several tense minutes, and repeated threats to clear the court, order was restored. The judge upheld the ruling of the jury, and the case was closed.

Once the verdict and the amount were read, I hung my head in defeat. Not only had I lost a major moral battle; I had also suffered a massive financial defeat. We quickly left the court, passing the media without comment. In the background I could hear Mrs. Jones and Dr. Johnson praising the verdict, and at the same time, denouncing it. It seems they had accepted the jury's finding of civil rights violations but were bitter that the jury did not adequately compensate for the loss of Calvin and Curtis.

As we drove away, Alice assured me that we could appeal the court's decision and, at the very least, delay any financial restitution, for months, if not years. She went on to talk about Florida's liberal bankruptcy laws and how we could legally walk away from the court's ruling for mere pennies on the dollar. I really wasn't listening; I could only visualize all my hopes and dreams of providing for Stacey spinning down the proverbial toilet.

Traci, Terry, Alice, and Robyn all tried to console me, but to no avail. Even Stacey tried to distract me by talking about school, and boys. That night, I didn't sleep. To make matters worse, I did something that I hadn't done in a long time; I got fall-on-your-face drunk.

Terry's Idea

At some point in the night, Terry had an epiphany. He called me immediately, but I was so drunk that I, honestly, don't remember the call. He also called Alice the next morning, and thankfully, she understood the idea. Alice spent the rest of the morning working the phones lining up a press conference for the following week.

Terry showed up around 9 AM to pick me up; dumbfounded, I said I didn't know what the hell he was talking about. Not one to give up easily, Terry got me moving and plied me with coffee to shake out the cobwebs from the night before. He said that we had many stops to make before the press conference next week and that we couldn't waste any time. Stacey, Terry, and I traveled to a local bank to talk with the manager. The bank did not want us to publicly use their name, but they would set up an account per Terry's request.

Next stop was an accountant, and then a lawyer, both highly recommended by Alice, and the details of Terry's wild idea were slowly working their way back into my mind. We worked with a web designer to bring Terry's idea to life, and then he went to the Post Office. I didn't know that they still had actual Post Office locations, but once inside Terry secured a P.O. Box for his grand idea. I thought the Post Office was just a waste of time, I mean who uses mail anymore for anything? In hindsight, I'm glad that Terry took this extra step. Everything was finished just in time for the press conference.

When we arrived at the appointed location, I saw a lot of familiar faces, my mom and dad, Officer Rodriguez and his family, and a host of other friends and supporters. Terry, Stacey, and I walked up to the makeshift podium to a round of applause. Terry began to speak—,

"Thank you, ladies, and gentlemen, of the press, for coming on such short notice. And thank you also Officer Rodriguez, and your family, for supporting David in his time of need. Last week's verdict was a serious setback to the financial future of David and his daughter Stacey.

"I've known David for several years now, and I know that if he had the money, he would gladly pay it to end this chapter of his life. However, I also know that since this whole drama began, David has not been able to work. At first, it was because of the injuries he had suffered, and the rehabilitation required to repair the damage caused by the *incident*. After that, his employer decided that David was too much of a public relations liability to continue working for them.

"Currently, the media attention has made it impossible for David to find a position with any company. So, as a result, there is the very real possibility that David will be forced to sell his home, his car, and all his possessions in order to pay just a small portion of the financial compensation as required by the court's decision. In effect, the court has ruled that David and Stacey would have to move in with family, or friends, to avoid becoming homeless.

"We cannot, in good conscience, allow this to happen.

"After discussing this dilemma with Alice Miller, David's Attorney, Officer Rodriguez and his family, and several other close friends and supporters of David and Stacey; we have decided to follow David's example and decisively act to avert this tragedy.

"We, David's friends, and family, have organized a relief fund to pay for the legal bills and the court ordered restitution. Everyone that you see here today has decided to give David all that they can, and more, to show our appreciation. We ask that you do the same. Please visit our website, *helping-david-dot-com* for information about this important effort. Or, if you prefer, please send any amount you can to David Taylor Relief Fund; P. O. Box one-two-eight-three-four, Orlando, Florida, thank you for your support."

Terry's idea was a deceptively simple plan, but how much it would help remained to be seen. I had thought that maybe we might get $50,000 total, but I had seriously underestimated the general public's sentiment. By the end of the week, we had raised more the $175,000.

Terry continued his public awareness crusade, speaking to radio talk shows, reporters, or anyone who could get the word out to the public. Within a month we had raised just over $1,000,000. Most of what came in was in the $10 to $20 range, but we also received larger amounts. Nothing, however, compared to what we were about to receive.

One day, while opening the multitude of envelopes, Terry came across one with a check for $1,000,000. At first, Terry thought that it was a joke, but then he read the note included:

Dear David

I recently saw your story on TV, and it touched me. Four years ago, I lost my only child when she was shot and killed by a gang member.

She was just an innocent bystander hit by a stray bullet, someone in the wrong place at the wrong time. The man responsible was charged and convicted, but nothing could erase the pain that I felt. Then I saw your story and realized that, while no amount of money can bring my daughter back, my wealth could help you and your daughter in your moment of need. Please accept the enclosed check as a token of my gratitude, from one father to another. Enjoy the precious moments today with your daughter; don't wait until tomorrow because we never know what tomorrow might bring.

John

Also included was a phone number and address, in California, with instructions to contact John if we ever needed anything else. Terry called the bank and verified the funds; it was a legitimate check. Terry called me immediately with the news, I said that there must be some mistake; he must have meant to write the check for $1,000. Terry was adamant that this was for real and urged me to call John.

I just had to be sure, so before we deposited the check, I called him. After a man answered the phone, I identified myself and asked if I was speaking to John. He replied that yes, he was John, and that he was glad to hear from me. We spoke for a while; he reassured me that the amount on the check was correct, and that more would be provided if needed.

He went on to ask about my employment prospects. When I told him that there were none, he offered me a job as a "consultant" for twice what I had made at my previous job. When I told him that I didn't want to take his money, he cut me off in mid-sentence, "Do it for Stacey, not for me."

When I told him that I didn't feel right being paid for doing nothing, he said that my most important job was being a father, and that I couldn't do that properly without a steady income. I told John that I needed some time to consider his offer; he said to take all the time that I needed.

That night I spoke with Stacey; her only question was if we would have to move to California. I told her that I didn't think so. Stacey told me to take the job, so to speak, and to find a way to meaningfully contribute to John and his company.

The next day, I made the call and told John I would accept his offer on two conditions: first, I would have to do something tangible to earn my salary, and second, I didn't want to move to California. John agreed to both stipulations and, suddenly, I was once again gainfully employed.

The War of Words

Now that the trials were over, I could address that thorn in my side— Dr. Johnson. Many times, Dr. Johnson had requested a public debate, but I would never consent. A point that Dr. Johnson felt necessary to exploit, every single chance he got. The time had come for me to finally face Dr. Johnson.

Knowing full well that I could not compete with his verbal skills, I decided to take a different approach, the written word. My idea was to respond to Dr. Johnson's insipid attacks utilizing the local paper's editorial column. My first attempt was in the form of an open letter to the editor:

Dear Editor,

My name is David Alan Taylor. Ever since the "incident" that I was involved with, Dr. Johnson has consistently labeled me a racist and an idiot. And on many occasions, Dr. Johnson has challenged me to a public debate; a debate that he would easily win. To Dr. Johnson, I would say this: I may be an idiot, but I am not stupid.

You, sir are an accomplished public speaker craving the attention of the masses, and I, on the other hand, am just a shy person with no desire to be in the spotlight, but to continue to ignore your character assassination would be a larger mistake on my part. So, if you want to really discuss race relations in America, then let's do it using a form of expression that we both can utilize, the printed word.

Admittedly, racism does still exist, but to blame everything bad that happens to blacks on racism is, well, to put it mildly, lunacy. Sometimes, bad things happen to bad people; unfortunately, sometimes, bad things happen to good people. Racism, however, is not the biggest problem facing blacks today. Black on black crime, as well as drug and alcohol addictions, constitute a serious threat to the black community. It is my opinion that people spouting rhetoric like you, regardless of race, are an even greater danger to black society than any cross-burning white supremacists could ever be.

Sadly, though, whites are not the only ones capable of racism. Blacks are also guilty of racist activities. An example would be the black community's reaction to the events surrounding my incident. Many black people accused me of racism, just because the dead and wounded were black, and I am white. Race, however, never played a role in my decision to shoot.

Unfortunately, there is a great chasm that divides 'white' and 'black' America. The geographical, political, economic, and social divisions that exist in society today feed this chasm. The only way to ever bridge this great divide is through inclusion and tolerance. You sir, however, subscribe to a different point of view. Your inflammatory orations seek to exploit our differences and prey upon our deepest fears.

You sir, perpetuate the racial differences by suggesting that 'white America' is somehow to blame for everything that befalls the black community. You offer up whites as a scapegoat, a sugarcoated placebo if you will, but you never address the real symptoms of a fractured society. You sir are the cause of the disease, not the cure.

People like you, white or black, who preach a spiteful message should be ignored, or at the very least, be looked upon with scorn. I urge both sides of the debate to reach a simple conclusion: we are better together than we are apart.

Sincerely,

David Alan Taylor

It wouldn't take long for Dr. Johnson to fire back. He wrote a fiery response, questioning my sanity, my morals, and my motivations. I, in turn, responded with another written attack; and so, it went, back and forth between Dr. Johnson and me. We fought many a heated battle, a prolonged war of words. In the end, however, neither one of us could claim victory.

My last response said I had decided the editorial debate was getting us nowhere. I argued the point, how can you make progress when one side of the debate refuses to accept valid facts presented by the other? How can you justify a position when you are unwilling to consider objecting opinions? Perhaps it was best if we should both agree to simply disagree. Dr. Johnson wasn't so gracious, he claimed that a great moral victory had been won, and his beliefs had been vindicated.

Yet, with John's generous contributions, I had more than enough money to cover my financial obligations to Mrs. Jones. Alice and I publicly announced that we would donate all excess funds, as well as any additional contributions that came in.

We were looking for a local group that would work exclusively in the black community located near Parramore Street. Traci, Terry, and I looked at several worthy organizations and non-profit groups that met our basic criteria, but we did not find an exact match. And then one day, Alice's office received a call from Theo Roberts.

Theo had an idea that he thought would work perfectly with our goals. Theo wanted to set up a community outreach program offering a variety of services to the Parramore Street area. He wanted to provide services such as free extended hours childcare, a modern computer room, workout areas, and an organized basketball league. Basically, Theo wanted to offer a safe place that young blacks could go to, and thus avoid the dangers of life on the street.

The idea sounded great, so we arranged a meeting. At the meeting, we worked out the basic details. Now armed with the proper financial backing, Theo would research a location and provide a projected budget. Finding the location turned out to be easy; there was an empty warehouse on the corner of Parramore and Central.

The size was perfect for Theo's needs, and the owner was willing to lease the property for a fraction of its market value. Next, we worked on finding a construction company that would assist with the building renovations. This too, turned out to be easier than expected. We found several companies willing to provide materials, equipment, or manpower, all at or below operational costs. Next, we worked with several companies to provide gym equipment, computers, and other necessities. Again, we found several companies that were willing to work within our budget constraints.

Everything was shaping up nicely; however, we were beginning to run low on money. I did not want to ask John for any more money, so we sought both public and private donations from a variety of sources. We were able to secure a grant from the state for the vast majority of our annual operational expenses. We also approached several of Orlando's rich and famous, producing mixed results. We met with many who were receptive to our financial needs, but some had no interest in our project at all.

One of those fitting into the latter category was Mrs. Jones. Since receiving her money, Mrs. Jones had moved from the Parramore district to a nice townhouse in Winter Park. She soon stopped talking to old friends, instead preferring to make new acquaintances with affluent black people, not white, that were more in line with her new image. I didn't have the nerve to ask her for money, but Theo did. He was bluntly told that she had no interest in the project.

Even without Mrs. Jones' assistance, we were able to secure enough money to cover the projected budget for the first two years. We named the completed project, appropriately enough, Theo's Place. Although it would take several months to complete, Theo's Place was an instant success story in the neighborhood.

Theo had individual rooms within the converted warehouse, named and dedicated to the memory of Calvin and Curtis Jones, Marcus Porter, and William Baker. Theo had been concerned that I might be offended by the suggestion, but he explained that he wanted the kids to know what can happen when someone makes bad choices in life. I said that it was his project, and that I had no objection to the dedications.

We held a naming ceremony prior to the official opening. Several members of the media, some low-level city officials, players from the *Orlando Magic,* and little old me, attended the ceremony. Notably absent, however, were both Mrs. Jones and Dr. Johnson, due to a '*scheduling conflict.*'

As expected, my presence caused a minor disturbance. Many people from the neighborhood still harbored a deep hatred of me; so, there were plenty of boos and hisses from the crowd. Theo immediately addressed the hostility.

"This day, this place, was only made possible by my friend, David Taylor.

"How we met is not important, what matters to me is what we do today. And today, we open this center so that no child in this neighborhood ever suffers the same fate of Calvin Jones, Curtis Jones, Marcus Porter, or William Baker.

"We, David and I, want every child in this neighborhood to succeed in life. And that starts with a safe place to just be a child. Someplace free of the drugs and the violence that plagues our neighborhood, someplace where parents can turn to when things get tough.

"Yes, David shot me, and the others…but I would not be here today, doing what I want to do for this neighborhood, without David's direct assistance. And you should recognize that effort, no matter how you feel about what happened that night.

“So, for those of you booing David’s presence, I ask you this; who else is here, supporting you today?

“The Mayor, your Congresswoman, the Governor? Nah, each one of them declined to be here…but David, he insisted on being here. Knowing full well how you would react, he still insisted on being here.

“If that doesn’t mean something to you, then you are all a bunch of fucking idiots.”

Homesick Stacey

By now school had begun, and though Stacey had made some new friends, she wasn't really happy. I could tell that something was bothering her, but I didn't know what. I kept asking her what was wrong, and all she would say was nothing. Finally, one night Stacey confided in me that she was homesick; she missed her old friends. I asked her if she wanted to go back to New York and live with Grandpa Jerry. She said that she didn't want to leave me now that we were together. Stacey liked Florida, but she just missed being in New York.

This left me in a difficult situation; should I stay here in Orlando, or do the rash thing and move to New York? I know it was a crazy idea, but when you're a father, you will do just about anything to make your daughter happy. I discussed the idea with Terry, who thought that a change of scenery might do me good.

Robyn, on the other hand, didn't like the idea of me moving so far away. My parents also were against a move to New York. Mom said that they don't see me much now when I only live five miles away. She couldn't imagine how often that she would see me if I moved to New York.

Gathering up the courage to discuss my dilemma with Traci was, at best, a slow process. We had become very close, but sometimes, I just couldn't find the words to express myself. To be more accurate, it wasn't my lack of words; it was an absence of faith in my words. Self-doubt and fear of rejection were character flaws that had developed deep roots into my psyche.

One night, though, after a few too many glasses of wine, I mustered up the strength to mention the subject. To my surprise, Traci was also facing a crisis of faith. It seems that a couple of weeks earlier, Traci had been approached by a network executive. He had seen her work regarding my story and wanted to offer her a job previously, but no openings were available at the time. Very soon, however, a position would be available, and he felt that Traci would be an ideal match. It turns out that Traci didn't know how to ask me about New York because, she too, was afraid that I would reject her.

We decided that it couldn't hurt to at least go and look at New York. Traci, Stacey, and I left on a Friday morning, just so we could get a glimpse of what New York life would be like. I had to admit, it was very different from what I was used to in

Orlando. When it was time to leave for Orlando, I found myself wanting to stay a little longer; and so did Traci. At that moment, we realized that a tough decision had just been made.

When we returned to Orlando, I let everyone know our decision. Terry thought it was great; now he would have a place to stay when he wanted to go New York. Mom cried and let me know how disappointed she was, but in the end, she accepted my decision. Dad asked, couldn't it be anyplace but New York? My Grandfather being originally from Boston, Dad never liked anything about New York. Robyn was both happy and sad; she had gotten used to my presence whenever she needed me, and now things would be different. I assured her that I would always be there for her, no matter how far away I was physically.

I asked Robyn, one last time, to join me; I said that we could make a new start, a new life far away from all the things that have conspired to keep us apart. Robyn may have been tempted, but she didn't show it; she said that she had to see how things would work out with Tom first. I reminded her that there was always a chance, and that any time she wanted to make a change; all she had to do was ask.

Before I knew it, we were in New York. We rented a place in Stacey's old neighborhood, so she could be near her friends and go back to the same school. I missed Orlando, or to be more exact, I missed Robyn. This was the first time in a while that we had not been able to meet anytime or anywhere that we wanted. Robyn and I spoke on the phone, almost daily; and it was always hard to say goodbye. I would remind her of my invitation to come check out New York, but she still wasn't ready to take a leap of faith. It's funny how a love can be so true, and yet, so wrong. It is tragic how two people, so perfect for one another, cannot find a way to be together.

Well aware of my feelings for Robyn, Traci didn't hesitate to show her displeasure. It wasn't the specter of Robyn hanging over our relationship that Traci objected to; it was my closeness to Robyn that Traci couldn't stand. I am ashamed to say it, but on more than one occasion, Traci and I fought about my feelings for Robyn. We would, however, manage to put my past behind us.

Eventually, I realized that Robyn would always be a part of my heart, but that part of me could not replace the love that I felt for Traci. Sometimes, I could be such an idiot, as Traci often reminded me, but not stupid. I was able to finally make peace with my conflicted heart, and I learned to enjoy the present. Robyn may have been my past, but Traci was my future; a future that I wanted so desperately to savor.

Two Years After the Event

It's been two years since the *incident* happened. With the move, I thought that the saga would now be over. However, something unexpected happened that made me reevaluate my reasoning. Long before moving to New York, I was approached by a publisher, several actually, interested in writing my story.

It appears that a little bit of fame, coupled with an intriguing story, is all you need to get a book deal these days. But what of the actual writing? Well, all the publishers said that they would take care of that part for me. I wasn't interested in someone else telling my story, so nothing came of the offers at the time. Yet, it got me thinking seriously about writing my own book. Sure, I had a little bit of fame, certainly an intriguing story, and a wealth of experience to draw upon. All I needed was some time to hone my writing skills.

Shortly after the event, my Dad recommended writing down my thoughts as a form of therapy. Ever since that day, I have been writing, and rewriting, my story. And then sharing each piece of my story with the people closest to me: Terry, Robyn, Traci, Randall, and Alice, to name a few.

Once I felt it was good enough to present to a publisher, I began the gut-wrenching process of submission. Eventually, I was able find the right publisher, and the end result will be the publication of this story. I am now in negotiations for the movie rights, and hopefully my story will be coming soon to a theatre near you.

Also, over the last few months, John and I started a PAC, FireArms Can be Terminal, or FACT. Our political goal is gun control legislation that makes sense. We are not anti-gun, but we are for several layers of restrictions, so that only responsible gun owners can legally possess firearms.

It was our belief that, in order to address the gun crisis happening in America today, we needed to focus on certain types of ammunition, select rifles, and an all-inclusive reduction of illegal handguns. Yes, FACT has become the proverbial David to the political Goliath, aka, the most powerful national gun lobbying organization (yes, that silly lawsuit still has not been settled). I now travel to Washington D.C. and talk to the very people who write and influence our laws: Senators, Congressmen, and the occasional former President.

Oh yeah, Traci and I are doing well. As a matter of fact, last month we decided to start talking about the possibility of getting married. I suppose that it didn't come as a surprise to those who are closest to us, but it was news to many others. We haven't decided if we will go through with that level of commitment yet, haven't even bothered to set a date, but if we do, I'll be sure *not* to tell the media.

Also, Stacey is adjusting very well to life with two celebrities, thank you very much. Approaching fifteen, Stacey is currently working hard on making all of my hair fall out. She's stubborn, insubordinate, and quite convinced that I have no idea what the hell I'm talking about. In other words, Stacey has "evolved" into a typical teenage girl.

So now you have the story of my life, thus far.

Do you think of me differently now, or have I confirmed your worst fears? Am I the monster that so many people have claimed me to be, or am I just a victim of circumstance?

Before you decide, remember that I am just like you. I am riddled with flaws, awash with hopes and dreams, and crippled by fears and desires. Like you, I'm just trying to stay afloat amid the maelstrom of life.

So, pass judgment now, if you must, but in all honesty, it doesn't really matter what you think of me. All that matters is what my friends, my family, and, most importantly, my daughter thinks of me. It's only taken me thirty plus years and one very public *incident* to figure that out.

Of course, there are times that I wish anonymity would just swallow me up again, but I know that will never happen. Thanks to the insatiable appetite of a media monster, I am now a permanent part of American History, albeit a brief footnote from a slow news day. Finally, after years of self-loathing and doubt, I like myself, and this Brave New World.

END

Special Acknowledgements

Funny how life places you where you need to be. There are so many people that I need to thank for supporting me when this book was nothing but a dream. First, she who shall remain nameless, thank you for pushing me out of the gravity that surrounded your world. To my wife, who doesn't quite understand this passion of mine, thank you for pulling me back to Earth and keeping me grounded while I followed this unorthodox path in life.

To Terry, I love you like a brother. You've always been there for me, and I appreciate it more than you will ever know. To my family, thank you for believing in me, even when I did not. To Paul and Lisa, words cannot express the gratitude that I have for your guidance over the last few years. This book, quite literally, would not have happened without your assistance.

To TAZ, you set me on this journey so many years ago and I am a better person for knowing you. Without you, none of this would have been possible. With you, none of this would have been necessary.

And, finally, to Sir Paul McCarthy, for singing the words that will live forever inside my heart:

"When I find myself in times of trouble
Mother Mary comes to me
Speaking words of wisdom
Let it be.

"And in my hour of darkness
She is standing right in front of me
Speaking words of wisdom
Let it be..."

About the Author

Henry D. Trett is an American author, artist, and entrepreneur. In addition, Mr. Trett has the unique honor of being the oldest of three children, and, oddly enough, also the youngest of five.

Curious how that works, huh?

An Orlando native, Mr. Trett currently resides in the Southeastern region of the United States with his wife, three dogs, eighteen koi fish, and a tortoise named Lucky.

Coming Soon by Henry D. Trett

HERO OF YESTERDAY?

CPSIA information can be obtained
at www.ICGtesting.com
Printed in the USA
BVHW031930281122
652963BV00008B/124

9 781959 715009